DEEPSEA UNDER THE POLE
GHISLAIN BARDOUT

GEOLOGIST FRANCESCO SAURO

PERPETUAL PLANET

For Rolex founder Hans Wilsdorf, the world was a living laboratory – the source of exploration, creation and inspiration. He used it as a testing ground for his watches, taking them to the most extreme locations, supporting the explorers who ventured into the unknown. Rolex continues his legacy with the explorers of today on their new mission: to make the planet perpetual. By supporting those who protect the oceans, study the effects of climate change and create a more sustainable world. Rolex stands behind the scientists, explorers and visionaries who will spark the imagination of future generations. Alone we can go far. But only together can we make the planet perpetual.

Discover more on rolex.org

#Perpetual

ROLEX

TF Design
Modern Designs in Resin

tf.design

Independent eyewear design handcrafted at the MYKITA HAUS in Berlin.
Camilla wears BRANDUR; Giulia wears BLU. Photography by Mark Borthwick.

Visit one of our MYKITA Shops in Bangkok, Barcelona, Berlin, Cartagena, Copenhagen, Los Angeles,
Monterrey, New York, Paris, Taipei, Tokyo, Washington, Zermatt and Zurich or shop online at mykita.com

MYKITA

Form *and* Function

Smooth checkouts, faster loading times and new
audio features, launching mid-June on *Kinfolk.com*

KINFOLK × Six

KINFOLK

MAGAZINE	EDITOR-IN-CHIEF	John Clifford Burns
	EDITOR	Harriet Fitch Little
	ART DIRECTOR	Christian Møller Andersen
	DESIGN DIRECTOR	Alex Hunting
	COPY EDITOR	Rachel Holzman
	FACT CHECKER	Gabriele Dellisanti
	EDITORIAL INTERN	Benjamin Tarp
	DESIGN INTERN	Bethany Rush

STUDIO	ADVERTISING DIRECTOR	Edward Mannering
	SALES & DISTRIBUTION DIRECTOR	Edward Mannering
	STUDIO & PROJECT MANAGER	Susanne Buch Petersen
	DESIGNER & ART DIRECTOR	Staffan Sundström
	DIGITAL MANAGER	Cecilie Jegsen
	CO-FOUNDER	Nathan Williams

STYLING, HAIR & MAKEUP

Jesse Arifien, Kirin Bhatty, Gaëlle Bonnot, Kelly Fondry, Andreas Frienholt, Helena Henrion, Katy Lassen, Antonio de Luca, Marquise Miller, Riona O'Sullivan, Nikki Providence, Ana Raquel Ribeiro, Sandy Suffield, Camille-Joséphine Teisseire, Nicole Wittman, Mélodie Zagury

WORDS

Alex Anderson, Rima Sabina Aouf, Amanda Avutu, Mark Baker, Eve Barlow, Katie Calautti, Stephanie d'Arc Taylor, Cody Delistraty, Daphnée Denis, Tom Faber, Bella Gladman, Harry Harris, Robert Ito, Ana Kinsella, Rebecca Liu, Stevie Mackenzie-Smith, Kyla Marshell, Megan Nolan, Debika Ray, Asher Ross, Charles Shafaieh, Ben Shattuck, Sharine Taylor, Pip Usher

PHOTOGRAPHY

Gustav Almestål, Luc Braquet, Francesco Brigida, Justin Chung, François Coquerel, Claire Cottrell, Pelle Crépin, Iringó Demeter, Brooke DiDonato, Jason Fenmore, Marsý Hild Þórsdóttir, Romain Laprade, Salva López, Emman Montalvan, Deedee Morris, Christian Møller Andersen, Daphne Nguyen, Vincent Pacheco, Sanjay Patil, Annelise Phillips, Pascal Silvain, Dominik Tarabanski, Benjamin Tarp, Esther Theaker, Aaron Tilley, Brian Venth, Cédric Viollet, Francesca Volpi, Dennis Weber, Corey Woosley, Yosigo

CROSSWORD	Anna Gundlach
PUBLICATION DESIGN	Alex Hunting Studio
COVER PHOTOGRAPH	Romain Laprade

Kinfolk (ISSN 2596-6154) is published quarterly by Ouur ApS, Amagertorv 14, 1, 1160 Copenhagen, Denmark. Printed by Park Communications Ltd in London, United Kingdom. Color reproduction by PH Media in Roche, United Kingdom. All rights reserved. No part of this publication may be reproduced, distributed or transmitted in any form or by any means, including photocopying or other electronic or mechanical methods, without prior written permission of the editor-in-chief, except in the case of brief quotations embodied in critical reviews and certain other noncommercial uses permitted by copyright law. The US annual subscription price is $87 USD. Airfreight and mailing in the USA by Worldnet Shipping Inc., 156-15, 146th Avenue, 2nd Floor, Jamaica, NY 11434, USA. Application to mail at periodicals postage prices is pending at Jamaica NY 11431. US Postmaster: send address changes to *Kinfolk*, Worldnet Shipping Inc., 156-15, 146th Avenue, 2nd Floor, Jamaica, NY 11434, USA. Subscription records are maintained at Ouur ApS, Amagertorv 14, 1, 1160 Copenhagen, Denmark. The views expressed in *Kinfolk* magazine are those of the respective contributors and are not necessarily shared by the company or its staff. SUBSCRIBE: *Kinfolk* is published four times a year. To subscribe, visit *www.kinfolk.com/subscribe* or email us at *info@kinfolk.com*. CONTACT US: If you have questions or comments, please write to us at *info@kinfolk.com*. For advertising inquiries, get in touch at *advertising@kinfolk.com*.

Starters

16 – 46

Features

48 – 112

"Use everything. Use all the styles that you like. Use the sad parts."
JENNY SLATE – P. 53

Photograph: Emman Montalvan

Movement

Directory

114 – 176

178 – 192

"I would even shake my head to the sound of the dog eating out of its bowl."
MARION MOTIN – P.117

Photograph: Pelle Crépin

PORTUGUESE
KNOWLEDGE
Flannel
IN A
NEW WORLD

WWW.PORTUGUESEFLANNEL.COM

In Japan, over 25 million people start the day with *rajio taisō*—a calisthenics class that has been broadcast to the nation via public radio since 1927. The mass exercise program is intended not only to improve fitness but also to create a regular moment of connection between the country's many islands. When we began putting together *Kinfolk*'s Movement issue, the idea of rajio taisō seemed quaint and almost nostalgic. As we finish the issue—working from our separate homes—it seems like a timely innovation once again. The spread of COVID-19 has forced us all to think differently about how we use our bodies. Where fitness centers close, streaming workouts boom; like participating in rajio taisō, logging into a remote workout class brings with it a sense of community.

The people interviewed in this issue have been chosen for the innovative ways they use movement in their exceptional careers. Conductor Roderick Cox treats it as a tool for communication, commanding whole orchestras with just the flick of a wrist. Champion skateboarder Alexis Sablone channels her unusual perspective on public space into her second career as an architect. Marion Motin, choreographer for Christine and the Queens and Stromae, dedicates her study of dance to what she calls "the immediate movement"—the impulsive and instinctive urges that grip us all from time to time. (As a child, Motin says she would shake her head rhythmically to the sound of her dog eating from its bowl.) And for those moments when life feels stagnant, birdwatcher Jason Ward reminds us of the sheer joy of watching the natural world move through the window: "Immediately, I'm like, it's not so bad... I'm not moving anywhere, but these birds are putting on a show and I'm enjoying it," he says.

Elsewhere, we turn toward summer and its tentative promise of liberation. From uncovering the mystery behind a picture-perfect pool to lamenting the lost pleasure of a diving board and defining the somewhat tame fashion for "wild" swimming, our contributors spent a lot of time with their toes in the water while researching stories for the issue. Should international travel still prove restricted over the summer months, flip to our fashion editorial on page 94—set on the volcanic, sea-sprayed shores of Madeira—for a breath of fresh air.

JOHN CLIFFORD BURNS & HARRIET FITCH LITTLE

expormim

1.

Starters

Designated Drudgery

How to take a load off.

You can't quite see the mental load the way you can see a pile of laundry or an armful of groceries, but that's part of the problem. Underpinning every household is a wealth of activity and thought that runs just beneath the surface, keeping everything from breaking down into chaos. What's in the fridge? Whose birthday is coming up next? How long have those dishes been there? The mental load is the endless to-do list of tasks and data that looms in the mind, a complex network of responsibilities that allows us to get anything done in the first place. In heterosexual relationships and family units, it generally falls to the woman.

Back in the 1990s, Dr. Susan Walzer, a professor of sociology at Skidmore College, identified what she termed "worry work." She interviewed 25 heterosexual couples about their experiences of the transition to parenthood and, in her paper *Thinking About the Baby*, observed that new mothers tended to find the feeling of ultimate responsibility for their child more stressful than their male partners did. "There were a couple of exceptional men in my sample," Dr. Walzer says. "But for the most part, worrying, processing information, and being the overall manager of care tended to fall to the women."

There are reasons for this: Women are encouraged to be caring from a young age, and society expects new mothers to have a natural inclination toward parenting that it doesn't necessarily pin on new fathers. But the mental load goes beyond families. In any close-knit group of people, be it a friendship group or a work cohort, one person is often identified as more thoughtful or capable, and as a result, an endless cycle of tasks will silently fall to that person. She books the group dinner or she organizes the cake for an office birthday. She looks up directions and she collects money for the upcoming weekend trip. Call her the burden-carrier, and let's always assume that she has had enough.

What if she simply stopped? This proposal works on the assumption that someone else will pick up the slack. In one week-long experiment conducted last year by Arielle Tchiprout, a *Cosmopolitan* journalist, the author's male partner fails to wake up in the morning when she skips the task of setting an alarm to wake him. He also elects not to purchase new toilet paper until they are down to the very last sheet. "We survived," he notes at the end of the week. His partner, drowning in a week's worth of unwashed laundry, fumes.

In fact, the range of proposed solutions available online—many of which revolve around feigned incompetence—would suggest that the problem is endemic in family units as well as workplaces and friendship circles. A *New York Times* article suggests that the way for the go-to person to step back is to become incapacitated through illness or injury for a prolonged period.

But avoidance—and engineering incapacitation—goes against the spirit of cooperation that is arguably fundamental to human progress, and if we can't rely on refusal, then it falls to us to redraft the rules. These issues often occur in groups that have well-established ties or a common goal—college friends or members of a team, for example. Perhaps remembering what brought you together can help lead to a solution. Dr. Walzer suggests strategies that focus on what is best for the group in the face of systemic unfairness. "Stay on the same team, resist enacting cultural notions of how families are supposed to work and try to be real about where the pleasures and needs actually reside," she advises. "In the end, we can't lecture or berate someone into wanting the best for us. But we tend to be willing to take on a lot for people we love—including making fair choices in an unfair context."
Words by Ana Kinsella

Monet's Cataracts

When great art meets modern medicine.

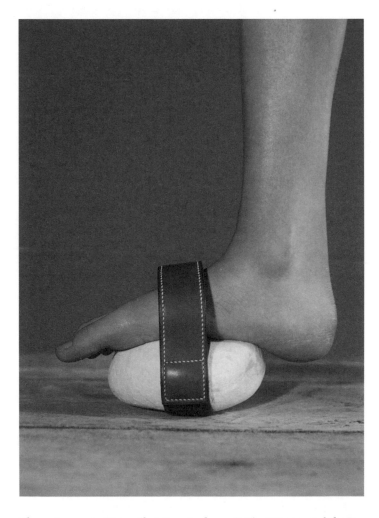

The princess in Hans Christian Andersen's *The Princess and the Pea* might have had fibromyalgia syndrome, according to two researchers in Stockholm. The chronic sleep disturbance and musculoskeletal pain common in FMS patients aligns with the restless nights that the fairy tale attributes to royal hypersensitivity. A princess is so delicate, the story goes, that even a little nub under a mountain of eiderdown would keep her awake. But the Swedish researchers say she wasn't just a spoiled royal, she was suffering.

Ours is the era of medical reasoning. Academic and neuroscientific publications have recently turned their gaze to the creative geniuses of the past, attempting to explain (or explain away) their rare insights. You might have heard that Nietzsche had stomach problems—irritable bowel syndrome, perhaps—that led him to detail larger existential suffering. There's a theory that Claude Monet painted blurry water lilies not because he was trying to upend the claustrophobic forms in romanticism by focusing on the immediacy of light and movement, but because he had cataracts. Francis Bacon's creative output could be attributed to dysmorphopsia—a condition in which a person is unable to correctly perceive objects (thus the swirl-faced portraits). Leonardo da Vinci sometimes depicted faces with one eye angled outward (a condition called exotropia); perhaps he had exotropia himself, which means he might have seen the world as flat.

Renoir had myopia. Rembrandt's self-portraits show a man whose eyes are angled slightly outward, technically called "stereoblindness." The condition might have allowed him to notice details that created the panoramic quality we admire in his paintings. Picasso founded cubism not to dismember 400 years of Western European painting tradition, one explanation goes, but because he had strabismus—he was cross-eyed, without clear depth perception, and so overcompensated on the canvas with bulky blocks. There was even a documentary in 2004 averring that Mozart had Tourette's syndrome, and that his use of complex arrangements was the result of his desire to control it.

These diagnoses all focus on impairment; they purport to show that personal adversity can lead to artistic greatness. But what do the revelations (most of which are unproven) really demonstrate? What can medical analysis offer? Consider the story of Einstein's brain: After the century's most famous genius passed away, his brain was extracted, sliced up and made into a thousand microscopic slides, then analyzed for traces of genius—however that would look. The slides revealed nothing of note and were shelved. The dominant theory emerged that he was just particularly good at connecting the dots—that he was, in short, an extremely creative person with a very high IQ.

Like with Einstein, at the heart of these postmortem diagnoses is an interrogation of creativity: Where does it come from, and is it real or just an accident baked into the body and mind of the creator? The explanation certainly could be in the way an eye is tilted or bowels are irritated. But perhaps it remains something more elusive—too complicated and multifaceted to be seen—no matter how powerful the microscope or elaborate the diagnosis.

Words by Ben Shattuck

Just a Minute

The trickery of online queues.

JOG ON

by Harriet Fitch Little

Before the invention of the sports bra, women found imaginative solutions to minimize the discomfort of exercising—like wearing bras two sizes too small or placing bathing suits on top of them. It took until the 1970s, when jogging became popular and the US enshrined equal access to college sports into law, before anyone thought to create women's underwear specially designed for movement. Supports for men were already widely available: In fact, the prototype for the Jogbra, the first sports bra to enter widespread circulation, was created by sewing two jockstraps together. Today, thankfully, the world is more supportive; even a mass-market sports bra is now precision engineered from around thirty different pieces of material.

"Good design is honest." So reads number six of the Ten Principles of Good Design, as carried down the mountain by revered industrial designer Dieter Rams. But it's a principle that software designers seem to disregard, especially with one innocuous-looking feature of our digital lives: the progress bar.

Downloading, uploading, buffering, processing, progressing—this is the terrain of the progress bar, a symbol that an action is underway and we are at some quantifiable distance from its completion. We might encounter these glyphs when "standing" in a virtual queue, or filling out an online questionnaire. On a small scale, they cater to two very human impulses: to imagine a goal, and then to accomplish that goal. It's why people love crossing items off to-do lists or clearing a line of Tetris blocks.

Progress bars have long been a software standard. A 1985 paper found that people overwhelmingly preferred to see some kind of "percent-done indicator" while a program carried out a task. (Imagine the alternative—a blank screen. It would likely prompt terror and boredom in equal measure.) Of course, we rarely have to wait for a computer to complete a task these days. It's more likely to be waiting for us. A couple of years ago, a journalist at *The Atlantic*, beguiled by the elaborate progress graphics of his tax return app, opened the source code and found it was an animation that played identically regardless of the user's inputs and without reference to what the software was actually doing at the time. Significantly, the animation also took longer than the computer's task did. But users didn't trust an app to crunch crucial, complicated numbers on the spot. In incorporating a delay, the app makers engaged in a design quirk that's been termed "benevolent deception"—a white lie users tend to welcome.

In this tender moment in tech, it's Rams' fourth design principle that perhaps shines a light: "Good design makes a product understandable." Harmless deceptions are fine, and in a few years, today's likely won't be necessary. But to get there, it helps to have designs that simplify, elucidate and educate.

Words by Rima Sabina Aouf

Kelly Carrington

A conversation with a doula.

With nearly two decades as a massage therapist under his belt, Kelly Carrington was already well-versed in the human body when, in 2014, he became Canada's first certified male birth doula. The father of three explains his part in the fast-growing maternity movement. *Interview by Pip Usher*

PU: *Doulas seem to be increasingly popular these days. Why?* **KC:** People are more educated about the birth process now. They want to have control because control feels safer. Sometimes they feel that having a doula will help give their birth a more team approach, rather than just going into the hospital as another patient.

PU: *What's the first thing that happens when you sit down with a pregnant woman?* **KC:** Most people will come to me at around 20 weeks and then we have two prenatal sessions in which we go through all the things that are in their little "box." This box is full of fear and anxiety and questions. We unpack that box so that, by the time the baby comes, it's empty and you can put a baby in it. I'm there for the birth and then we have a plan in place for postpartum care afterward.

PU: *How do you establish the sort of bond that means a family trusts you at their most vulnerable moment?* **KC:** I listen. I understand that it's an odd situation where they're inviting a complete stranger into their lives for a very short period of time so we have to become fast friends. I need my clients to feel as comfortable as possible with me—and it's not just the mom, the partner has to feel comfortable, too. Because when it's go time, I don't want me being there to be detrimental to the cause.

PU: *Do you experience friction between the hospital environment and your work as a doula?* **KC:** No, because I'm not there to do their job and I make sure those boundaries don't get crossed. I'm not a wallflower: I'm a 215-pound black man with dreadlocks. I can't just blend into the room. But I'm there to support the family, and I try to make my presence as unobtrusive to the medical staff as I can.

PU: *Does the role of a doula end at birth?* **KC:** I'm there to follow the family for as long as they require. My motto has been, "I'm your doula until you tell me otherwise," so it's a pretty good deal. I'm your doula for life! If you put this commitment in monetary terms, I don't make any money. But it's not about that; it's about helping people get to the end of this process—especially the labor and delivery and postpartum part—with confidence. It's about empowering them, however long that takes.

PU: *Could the role of doula be applied to other key moments in life, like death?* **KC:** The most stressful times in your life are most likely to be when you get married, when you have a baby, when you buy a house, and when you're about to die. When you buy a house, you have a Realtor; when you're about to get married, some people have a wedding planner. When people call themselves a "bereavement doula," all they're really doing is supporting a family through a situation.

A WOMAN'S WORK?
by Pip Usher

Because doulas have historically been women, Carrington knows he's a "bit of a show pony." To avoid being a novelty hire, he encourages families to also interview other prospective doulas to make sure he's the right fit. Such conscientiousness extends to every stage of the process, from ensuring that the partner doesn't feel threatened by his presence, to making adjustments for women concerned about nudity. "I've had moms before that were very concerned about their backside being exposed during labor," he explains. "I said, 'Okay, no problem, I'll just follow you around with a blanket.'" Ultimately, though, he finds his gender has less bearing than you'd think: "It's the intention that's the most important thing."

Left Photograph: Iringó Demeter, Right Photograph: Deedee Morris

WILD THINGS

by Stevie Mackenzie-Smith

In 1996 the British writer Roger Deakin decided to swim his way around the British Isles, starting the journey from the murky Elizabethan moat on his farm. His chilly adventure had transformative effects. "When you enter the water, something like metamorphosis happens," he wrote in *Waterlog*, the 1999 book chronicling his odyssey. In the 21 years since, *Waterlog* has become something of a bible to proponents of "wild swimming": an adrenaline-raising trend nudged into popularity by its publication.

But why call it "wild"? Perhaps it's because we've domesticated the act and become accustomed to man-made pools. In swimming pools, you can see what lies beneath. But in a river, it's all left to the imagination, for better or worse. In our sanitized lives, as we contemplate ways of "resisting the attention economy," we're slowly finding our way back into open water with all its unchlorinated possibilities.

In *Swimming Studies*, writer and artist Leanne Shapton likens freshwater swimming to "the warmth of a slap." For many wild swimmers, this novel shock is why they keep getting in. The initial gasp of submersion is a shortcut to becoming deeply attuned to what's around us. That might be the feel of toe-licking algae or the shrieks of the teenagers that always know a watering hole better than anyone else. In London, to swim at the Hampstead Ponds has become a slightly self-satisfied shorthand for cultured taste. But at its core, outdoor swimming is a humbling pastime, and like all good hobbies, a brilliant way of doing nothing at all. *Photograph by Jason Fenmore*

A SHOO-IN

by Harriet Fitch Little

We don't begrudge athletes their natural advantages, but what about their high-tech gear? As sports technologies become ever-more sophisticated, the idea of "mechanical doping" is hitting the headlines. For example, most marathon-running milestones in recent years have been achieved by athletes wearing versions of Nike's Vaporfly: candy-hued sneakers in which scooped soles act like tiny springboards and reduce the energetic cost of running by approximately 4%. Those not sponsored by Nike have called it cheating, but others see it as a natural evolution of the sport—including the World Athletics committee, which recently ruled that the spring-loaded shoes would be allowed at the Olympics. If it's okay for the professionals, you can certainly use high-tech activewear in good conscience to shave a few minutes off your park run.

Triple Threat

Why do good things come in threes?

The third drink is the best, allowing us to dance freely and shoot gorgeous pool. (The fourth does us in.) Three brothers Karamazov, three brothers Marx, the Three Musketeers, three little pigs, three blind mice, three-course meals.

Three of something seems complete. It's a number that holds an almost magical power over the human mind. And when we encounter something too complex or messy to understand, our first instinct is to split it into three parts. Young writers tend to group their adjectives in threes—a habit that is sleepy, predictable and comforting. Threes are everywhere in Shakespeare ("Tomorrow and tomorrow and tomorrow…"), and form one of the most common rhythmic devices in poetry. Riddles, too, are best in threes. Think of Oedipus and his Sphinx. When it comes to luck, three times is said to be the charm, though bad things are also rumored to come in threes. Since the bombing of Hiroshima, we've known that a third world war would be the last.

Why are trios so easy to remember? It may be developmental—that stemming from a saturation of threes in nursery rhymes and picture books our minds grow to expect them. But it could also be our natural affinity for a basic mathematical truth: We need at least three instances to see a pattern. Pattern recognition is an elemental part of cognition. It's what makes us grin as the third line of a joke approaches. Threes give the mind a sense of control, of having something to work with. And that's why they are a stock-in-trade for all the consultants, teachers, motivational speakers and trial lawyers who would like us to remember three simple things when we go home today. We will.

Three witches, three wishes, three strikes and you're out. Three items make a list, three acts a play, three missed calls an emergency. The returns of kings and Jedis, all those beginnings, middles and ends. We crave the third and final installment, and always have. Without it we wait, and wait, and…

Words by Asher Ross

Left Photograph: Brian Venth. Model: Yasmin Shaheed. Right Photograph: Sanjay Patil

Photograph: Francesca Volpi

That Syncing Feeling

The surprise joys of synchronization.

Every morning, in schoolyards and public parks, millions of Japanese people bend and stretch following directions recorded over a piano track—a nearly century-old fitness routine known as *rajio taisō*. These Japanese calisthenics date back to 1927, when the Ministry of Posts and Japan's public broadcaster, NHK, teamed up to promote national health exercises on the radio. According to the Japanese government, over 25 million people still participate in the three-minute-long choreography at least twice a week, enjoying the communal exercises "not only for their health benefits but also as an activity that brings people together."

Perhaps surprisingly, synchronized group gymnastics may foster cooperation, improve mental health and make people more sympathetic to one another. Whether it be dancing, exercising or even just tapping a finger at the same time as someone else, research shows that synchrony helps us bond with others, and makes us more likely to trust them as a result. In a 2015 study, experimental psychologists from the University of Oxford found that subjects coordinating their movements to a rhythmic beat raised their tolerance to pain and felt closer to the group they were with. Prior studies have established that moving in sync boosts our self-esteem, enhances our sense of trust and makes people we interact with more memorable. Even virtual synchronized interactions can make us feel better about ourselves and closer to the people we harmonize with.

In a time of growing individualism, the popularity of viral dance challenges as performed by teenagers imitating their favorite singers on the video-sharing app TikTok, real-life flash mobs or even group yoga sessions all highlight a natural inclination for falling into rhythm with one another. Marching to the beat of the same drum helps us form new bonds—regardless of what that drumbeat sounds like.
Words by Daphnée Denis

Kali Malone

According to Kali Malone, it's when her own compositions send her to sleep that they're ready for the public. But while her music is certainly meditative, some may struggle to drift off to the massive slabs of sound, austere drones and minimal melodies that bloom from the speaker and slowly take over the whole room.

After growing up in Colorado, Malone moved to Stockholm at 18 and studied electro-acoustic composition. Now 26, she has quietly taken the experimental music world by storm with her 2019 album, *The Sacrificial Code*—a two-hour-long series of mournful pipe organ compositions. When we speak on the phone, she's in Paris, where she's spending a few weeks recording in her dream studio. *Interview by Tom Faber*

TF: *Where are you working exactly?* **KM:** Ina GRM is a legendary studio that's part of Radio France. A lot of musique concrète and early electronics were made here.[1] They set me up for two weeks with a bunch of amazing old synthesizers that my idols once used. I feel very connected to a historical lineage working here. It's an honor.

TF: *Is this the experimental music you grew up on?* **KM:** Not quite. I grew up in Denver's vibrant underground, where there are lots of warehouse shows. I was exposed to a lot of experimental electronic music, punk and metal, but I didn't realize it all had an academic history until I moved to Sweden.

Photography: Luc Braquet

NOTES

1. Musique concrète uses preexisting sounds as its raw material. Pioneered by French composer Pierre Schaeffer in the late 1940s, the technique involves collaging together small bits of tape—often sped up, looped or reversed—to create entirely new compositions.

2. Many organs have pipes that emit low noises inaudible to the human ear. In controlled experiments, the presence of these bass notes has been found to elicit strange feelings—such as shivers down the spine—in a significant number of participants.

TF: *I don't immediately think of "punk" when listening to your music.*
KM: Oh really? I think I have a punk attitude. For music to be transgressive or punk it doesn't necessarily have to have thrashing, aggressive timbres in it. Punk is a social context. Music isn't just the organization of sound, it's a lot of complex social interactions piled on top of each other.

TF: *When you moved to Sweden, your social context must have shifted. Did your music change?* **KM:** I was 18 when I moved—every part of me was changing. Sweden is easier for musicians, there's more state support. It's different than America: There, you have to kick and scream just to do your thing, cops take away your community venues, the city's gentrifying and nobody can afford rent. You actually need each other to survive and that's often the grounds for creativity. In Sweden, you can be a freelance musician and have a semi-stable future. I never knew that was even an option in the States.

TF: *Your compositions are governed by strict rules. Why do they still sound so emotional?* **KM:** A lot of my music is inspired by the compositional structures of early church music, which is basically like algorithms. The reason that music is so powerful is because of its pattern structure and specific harmonic values. The church understood how to press the buttons in our brains that recognize extreme, beautiful proportions and manipulate us.[2] It's like grabbing a cat by the neck—we go all limp.

TF: *How do people outside the experimental niche respond to your music?* **KM:** I didn't think they heard my music until my last record, which even my grandma and five-year-old cousin liked. This is the first time people outside my circuit have said: "Oh yeah, this is music," rather than: "What are those weird sounds?" I think it's because of the harmonies.

TF: *Not because of you?* **KM:** I tend to push away magical thinking: I'm not sure that composers imbue their work with some special essence. No, it's just harmonic science: It's proportions and air that is wiggling. If you do that tastefully, it will reach people.

GROUPE DE RECHERCHES MUSICALES
by Harriet Fitch Little

The GRM (Groupe de Recherches Musicales) was founded by Pierre Schaeffer in the early 1950s to further composers' explorations of musique concrète. The GRM's Paris studio became a mecca for experimental musicians such as Karlheinz Stockhausen and Iannis Xenakis, who were keen to use its abundance of newly available audio and recording technology to manipulate sounds and create experimental compositions. In the 1970s, the studio embraced electronic music and attracted a new wave of musicians using early computer software to make their recordings. Today, the GRM continues to support cutting-edge artists such as Kali Malone.

For generations of schoolchildren, the diving board symbolized the delicious freedom of summer vacation. With no homework to distract, riotous chatter coalesced around diving towers in swimming pools. An impressive leap might be a means through which a swimmer could flirt or assert social standing. But for others, the magic was simply in the exhilarating, even transcendental freefall into the shimmering blue. How often can a kid experience that? Today, municipal diving boards are increasingly hard to find. Like many everyday activities, when a dive goes wrong, it can be fatal. And so since the 1970s, health and safety concerns, lack of investment and new diving regulations have led to a decline in the amateur pastime. As of 2015, there are just three public pools in New York City with diving boards. In London, swimming pools with diving facilities fell from over 96% to less than 10% between 1973 and 2003. This summer, why not seek out one of the last remaining diving boards for yourself? Will you lead with a goofy cannonball? Maybe a dive that starts with an elegant twist? The belly flop? Stretch your fingers to the heavens, and launch into the deep for the sheer fun of it.

Words by Stevie Mackenzie-Smith
—

Known Unknowns

Waiting for news—be it medical test results, exam grades or the outcome of a job interview—can be agonizing. Kate Sweeny is a professor of psychology at the University of California, Riverside, and one of her research topics is the mental impact of waiting for news: why it's so distressing, whether anticipation serves a purpose and what we can do to make the waiting period more bearable. Sweeny's advice is to distract yourself, stay grounded in the present moment and, above all, remember that you are not alone. She points out that she has "yet to meet a person who doesn't struggle with facing uncertainty in some way."
Interview by Bella Gladman

BG: *Why is waiting for news so unpleasant?* **KS:** Like most emotions, worry has a function: to keep your attention on avoiding future harm. Sometimes—with biopsy results or an election, say—your worry is telling you to act, but there's nothing you can do. There's really no way out of that, but we're trying to find ways to make it easier.

BG: *What can help?* **KS:** There are two things. Mindfulness is one of them. Waiting involves a lot of mental time travel: thinking back to how you could have avoided this situation, and inevitably worrying about the future. Mindfulness is about focusing on the present moment and not letting your thoughts totally carry you away. Regular practice makes people feel like they are coping better.

Another thing that has been shown to help is practicing activities that get you into "flow state," which is when you are so completely absorbed that the outside world disappears. It's a distraction from the pain of uncertainty. Such activities tend to be sufficiently challenging to absorb your attention. Video games are custom-made for this, as they get harder incrementally as you improve. This progress aspect might help in letting you feel more in control. Everyone has their own flow activities—my nerdy go-to is analyzing data! For others, it might be gardening or exercise. These coping mechanisms can't eliminate the pain of waiting for news—they're simply to get the worry to a tolerable level, where you can get a good night's sleep and take care of your life.

BG: *Is there any folk wisdom that's maddeningly wrong?* **KS:** About 10 years ago, "think positive" was on every magazine cover. It was getting absurd. People were saying you can think your cancer away. Clearly, that's problematic! Some of my research has focused on the benefits of *not* thinking positively. If you lower your expectations and become pessimistic in the final moments of waiting, it's actually beneficial. It prepares you for the worst, and as a side effect if things go well, then you feel even better. The good news is that almost everyone does this naturally.

BG: *What can givers of bad news do better?* **KS:** How best to minimize suffering for the recipient depends on the outcome you want. If your goal is to have the person feel as good as possible walking away, ending on some kind of high note is the way to go. The future is going to be great even though they didn't get the job, or whatever it is. However, if the goal is to get the person to do something about that news—like make lifestyle changes to combat high cholesterol, or study harder because they're failing a class—you want to end on a bad note. That can be hard, as everybody wants to buffer bad news in a positivity sandwich. We also need to be realistic about the fact that giving bad news will never be pleasant for either party—so be as clear as you can. The tendency to avoid having to give bad news is so strong that you can cover it up so much that it's not clear to someone that they've received bad news, which is a big-time recipe for bitterness and anger on the recipient's side.

BG: *How can we best support other people when they're waiting for news?* **KS:** There's a huge body of research on social support—there's no one-size-fits-all approach to being supportive. Your best chance is to just ask them what they need, and don't assume. You may be trying and feel like you're failing, but if you're there, you're probably doing better than you would if you'd just stayed away.

Phillip Youmans

The 20-year-old director talks to *Sharine Taylor* about walking the tightrope between teen prodigy and award-winning filmmaker.

Photography: Justin Chung, Styling: Marquise Miller

If Phillip Youmans had to describe the past few years in one word, he'd choose "blooming." "It really does feel like a period of tremendous emotional, personal and creative growth," he says, speaking on the phone from his current base in LA. That's to be expected from someone with Youman's CV: Last year he became the Tribeca Film Festival's youngest featured director and the first African American to receive the revered Founders Award with his debut, *Burning Cane*—a startling accomplishment for someone who, at the time the film was produced, was in their final year of high school.[1]

Burning Cane is a visually poetic character study of how a mother, her son and their pastor navigate personal demons against the backdrop of Louisiana's rural Baptist church. The film neither condemns nor shames faith but rather interrogates how it functions—and sometimes falters—in the lives of its parishioners, a question that loomed large for Youmans throughout his childhood in New Orleans.

Youmans is enrolled in NYU's film and television program and, while he says he still has his student ID in his wallet, he's pressed pause on his studies for now to pursue opportunities in LA. "I was staying in class more for what my family would think as opposed to what I thought, and that's really not a way to live," he says. "I don't see school, or a return to school, being part of the equation any time soon."

Living in California, Youmans is close to ARRAY—Ava DuVernay's distribution company, which was responsible for getting *Burning Cane* onto Netflix last year.

NOTES

1. *Burning Cane* began as a short script written during Youmans' junior year of high school. After financing principal photography with savings and crowdfunding, he contacted *Beasts of the Southern Wild* director Benh Zeitlin for assistance turning it into a feature.

2. Youmans' previous directorial projects include *Nairobi* (2019), a short film made with Saint Heron—Solange Knowles' creative agency—about a West African family's immigration to New York.
—
—

"I felt like that idea of having to climb up the ladder was a complete fallacy. You either have to take the chance now or never."

ST: *You acted before deciding to direct. Was there a moment that gave you the push that you needed to make the switch?* **PY:** It was a combination of things. The biggest was that I felt like a lot of the creative control I was interested in was on the other side of the camera. By being a director, I could have more control over my career. I've been writing plays since I was a kid, and I was acting in theater before I went into small roles in films, so I've always been fascinated by storytelling in general.[2] Another big realization came when I decided it was time to stop being a production assistant or gaffer on other people's sets. All those positions are incredibly important, but I realized that if I wanted to be a director, I had to make my own stuff and stop thinking about other people's work. I just felt like that idea of having to climb up the ladder—you have to start as a PA until you end up being a director—was a complete fallacy. That's not how it works at all. You either have to take the chance now or never.

ST: *Your approach to* Burning Cane *was informed by watching your own family navigate religion. What was it like translating that into a visual project? Did you find it cathartic?* **PY:** Definitely. The making of it was cathartic, but bringing it out to the world was another cathartic experience. I was forced not only to have that conversation with myself but also to confront my family in a very public way. Talking about this kind of stuff openly—talking about issues that for so long I just kept within and contained among my family—has brought us closer. In making this film, it definitely forced me to confront how and why people believe the things they do and why I'm in no position to judge.

I totally understand why it's important to believe, to have that emotional refuge, to have emotional solace when you don't know what lies beyond or if you can't find meaning. When I was younger, I was much more gung ho, much more of a jerk and an asshole [about religion]. It's just [a matter of] being more nuanced with the idea, more honest and more empathetic to why these things are important for people, whether I believe in them or not. I also had another realization: Kobe [Bryant]'s death really affected me. It forced us to confront our own mortality in a way, and it made me question, am I a religious person? No, not at all. Am I a Christian in a traditional sense? No, but I don't want to be definitive about something that I'm not sure about. I don't want to believe in oblivion.

ST: *It's interesting to hear you say you used to be "a jerk" about religion. With* Burning Cane, *you were compassionate but critical. Was that challenging?* **PY:** I wouldn't say it was challenging. I was aware of the process the entire way—of making sure that it felt authentic and like an invitation. But it's also easy because I grew up in it. It's easy to detect what felt like going too far, what felt like it was insincere. That was an important thing that I had to gauge constantly because the moment something moves into caricature or parody, then it's a completely different piece. It's a damnation or judgment and that's not what the film's about at all.

In unpacking religion—even outside of what it represents—it was important for me on a very fundamental level to recognize that despite all the love that you can find in some of the relationships you can build in that space, there is a lot of darkness that needs to be uprooted. Especially in terms of the antiquated, traditionalist, homophobic values. It's impossible to deny the fact that they're perpetuated in that space. It would be completely counterproductive to not recognize that that's part of the equation.

ST: *So much of pop and internet culture is created by teenagers, particularly black teenagers. Do you feel like people aren't giving young people due credit when they express surprise at the maturity of your film?* **PY:** At least from my perspective, I didn't feel like I had to draw from anything otherworldly. It didn't feel like anything foreign. I was fully aware of my age from the moment that we were making the project. All of my friends knew that people took us less seriously in production because we were younger, but we used that to our advantage. We got so many things for free and received so much help from the community because people just wanted to help us make a project.

ST: *It's early days, but do you ever think about your legacy?* **PY:** I want people to know that my intentions, at least for us and our stories, were always in the right place. As an artist, I try to create in the most selfless context possible all the time. I really do feel the weight of cultural responsibility, but I take that weight on in stride and in appreciation. Recently, I started to think about the responsibility that we have as artists and as artists of color. It's a responsibility that is not a burden in any way. It really is an honor.

Burning Cane was a representation of a cautionary, bleak perspective that I had grown up with and the conversations that I was having, but it is not indicative of the future or of the stories that I want to continue to tell. It was almost like emotional shedding. I felt like I had to get out of me. But I don't want my narrative or even my voice as an artist to be defined by such bleakness when there is so much beauty everywhere, especially in our experiences as black people.

Youmans' next feature-length project will focus on the New Orleans chapter of the Black Panthers in the 1970s.

WALK ON WATER

by Harriet Fitch Little

In 2016, the artist Christo created a three-kilometer-long walkway on Lake Iseo in northern Italy and invited the public to "walk on water"—or, rather, between islands and the mainland—via a system of piers wrapped in saffron-colored fabric. Initially conceived of by Christo and his wife and collaborator, Jeanne-Claude, back in the 1970s, *The Floating Piers* ultimately only came to fruition several years after Jeanne-Claude's death in 2009. Like the boardwalk or the boulevard, the walkway was free for all: "an extension of the street," as Christo put it.

Consider the Boardwalk

Where the city meets the sea.

If you'd been a child in the late 1800s, the Atlantic City boardwalk would have been a place of pure wonder. Racing across the wooden boards, saltwater taffy in hand, you could weave between the legs of big-city visitors and the rolling chairs, pushed by dapper attendants, in which the wealthy rode past grand hotels. Opposite Applegate's Pier was a carousel, mesmerizing crowds with its hypnotic revolutions and the siren song of its organ, piping out popular songs.

Though originally designed as a temporary solution to keep the sand out of seaside buildings, the boardwalk—a simple raised wooden walkway—is an American institution. It has supported the feet of revelers for 150 years—an iconic place to people-watch, buy a hot dog, check out a sideshow or ride a Ferris wheel.

New Jersey is the birthplace of the structure, offering entertainment by the sea all along the Jersey Shore. Atlantic City's boardwalk is the oldest, longest and grandest, even giving its name to the most expensive property on the Monopoly board. Boardwalks sprung up in imitation of it across the US, each with their own local flavor: fairground rides in Coney Island, stuntmen in Santa Cruz, bodybuilders and fortune-tellers in Venice Beach.

City dwellers flock to boardwalks when the routine of urban life can no longer contain them. Over decades, the entertainment has changed, but the boardwalk's chief draw is the same: the thousand moods of the ocean. Since beaches are often private property, boardwalks are an egalitarian space where anyone may enjoy the sea, but also a tool to keep man and nature separate, to parcel wildness into pretty views.

It's not all just about the fun and games on top of the boardwalk, however: The space underneath has long fascinated artists. In the crooner classic "Under the Boardwalk," the Drifters describe it as a place where lovers find some hard-sought privacy. And generations of photographers have documented that underworld of complex shadows, home to city detritus, encampments of homeless people and the occasional dead body.

The boardwalk's glamour was already fading by the middle of the 20th century, and by the 1970s many boardwalks had gone into decline. The soft, splintering wood of their walkways was often replaced by concrete. (When it was not, joggers occasionally fell through the rotting boards into pits of trash.) Gradually the word "boardwalk" became a byword for sin and decay. In fact, seediness was nothing new: Coney Island was once known as "Sodom by the sea," and the HBO show *Boardwalk Empire* details criminal machinations in the Prohibition era.

It makes sense that humans should flock to the threshold between civilization and nature: It's the eternal allure of life on the edge. But the boardwalk's permanence depends on the sea remaining a stable distance from the shore. Unfortunately, erosion is disfiguring shorelines and Atlantic City has one of the highest risks of flooding in the country. Major hurricanes in 1944, 1962 and 2012 destroyed boardwalks, which some cities elected not to rebuild. On the other hand, over the years, the boardwalk in Wildwood, New Jersey has been moved twice to bring it closer to the ocean. Like so much in America, the boardwalk is founded on a myth. It is built to help us stand unbowed beside the enormity and indifference of nature, to convince ourselves, however briefly, that it can be contained.
Words by Tom Faber

Far Left Photograph: © Christo, Left Photograph: Yosigo

A VERY PRIVATE POOL
by Harriet Fitch Little

Romain Laprade's image of a calm, sun-kissed swimming pool brings to mind the saying "still waters run deep": The photograph is actually the conclusion of a decades-long mystery. In 1976, Magnum photographer Martine Franck took a celebrated black-and-white photograph of a group of women relaxing on the decking of a sculptural pool in southern France. Franck's image became famous, but the location faded into obscurity. A few years ago, curators from the nearby Villa Noailles launched a detective mission to find its exact location using satellite imagery. They reasoned, rightly, that it wouldn't be hard to spot: "It was a huge pool surrounded by white," Laprade points out. Laprade was commissioned to photograph the newly located pool in 2017, and he was fortunate enough to meet its owner and creator, the architect Alain Capeilleres. "He was more than 90 years old and very proud to show us this unknown masterpiece," recalls Laprade, who describes the modernist creation as "one of the most incredible places I've seen." Laprade's images were displayed at Villa Noailles' annual architecture exhibition in 2018 to much acclaim; sadly, Capeilleres died shortly before the opening. Today, he remains a mystery. "He had no archives to show us, no pictures," says Laprade. Still, Laprade is proud that Capeilleres now has at least one of his creations documented for posterity. "He did not realize that he had created a masterpiece," he says. *Photograph by Romain Laprade. Courtesy of Villa Noailles.*

Here's an unimportant question for you: What is a single word for the intersection of three roads? The answer: trivium. Now, pluralize the word in the Latin way, and you'll have another bit of non-useful information: trivia.

Although trivia began as a geographical term, it came to denote the inconsequential information people exchange when bumping into each other at a trivium—bits of gossip or news that keep conversation short, cordial and interesting. In other situations, these trivialities became evidence of mental virtuosity, scraps extracted on demand from the vast store of data people carry around with them. Because some people seem to possess more facts than others—and readier access to them—a mental sport was born in pubs and living rooms everywhere. Contestants gleefully vie to dredge up useless historical details, bits of entertainment lore and scientific minutiae more quickly than their opponents. The reward is glory or cash—finally, a sure demonstration of the strange and ancient alchemy of turning something useless into gold.

Recently, almost 15 million viewers watched the *Jeopardy!* showdown in which Ken Jennings won $4 million in prize money and was crowned trivia's "greatest of all time." In one round on art, he and his rivals swiftly identified Jørn Utzon's 1957 contest-winning design (the Sydney Opera House), the painter of *The Screaming Popes* (Francis Bacon) and the art movement with which ceramicist Beatrice Wood was associated (Dada). The fun of watching is that you or I might also have the answers, and the alacrity to shout them out before anyone else.

Accessing lots of insignificant information isn't all idle entertainment, however. John Harris, a professor of literature at Brigham Young University, claimed that, unlike a specialist who "learns more and more about less and less, until he knows everything about nothing," a global thinker can synthesize all sorts of seemingly unimportant and unrelated data into a broad understanding of things. Harris maintained that there is no "such a thing as useless or trivial knowledge." So, hold on to those bits of trifling intelligence you've squirreled away; they are bound to come in handy at some point.

Words by Alex Anderson

Trivial Matters

On the uses of useless knowledge.

Photograph: Brooke DiDonato. Overleaf: Photograph: Merce Cunningham Dance Company, Scenario, by Timothy Greenfield-Sanders, 1997.

Aggravating Circumstances

What makes something annoying?

In this era of global chaos, it can be easy to forget that there are events that don't elicit extreme reactions such as despair, euphoria or terror, but have an emotional effect on us nonetheless. To remind you what that feeling is, consider the following: the noise emanating from your seatmate's headphones; someone standing a fraction too close to you in line; the website that takes forever to load. Ah yes, there it is—annoyance.

Are some things objectively annoying? Possibly. As Flora Lichtman, co-author of the 2011 book *Annoying: The Science of What Bugs Us*, suggested in an interview with NPR, there's something about the mix of frequencies that makes the sound of fingernails running down a blackboard intrinsically aggravating. "But that's sort of rare," she adds. "Most annoyances seem pretty personal." On the other hand, a 2009 study by Noah Eisenkraft and Hillary Anger Elfenbein described a concept called "affective presence." They found that those with a positive affective presence make others around them feel good, while those with a negative affective presence have the opposite effect. It's like your "emotional signature," Elfenbein told *The Atlantic*. She added: "To use everyday words: some people are just annoying."

Science has frustratingly few explanations for annoyance, but Lichtman and her co-author, Joe Palca, define it as something that's unpleasant without being harmful; unpredictable and intermittent; persistent for an uncertain period of time and contextually and culturally specific. All these characteristics point to annoyance being more about our own intolerance than about the objective qualities of the irritant itself. There's no real way to free yourself from the exasperating reality of a world full of people and things, so the emotion is ultimately futile. "Annoyances are intrinsic to modern human life and you're just going to have to deal with it," says Palca. Annoying, right?
Words by Debika Ray

Word: Frenemy

Worst friends ever.

Etymology: A portmanteau of the words "friend" and "enemy," frenemy is thought to have been coined in 1953 when American gossip columnist Walter Winchell suggested applying it to the fraught relationship between Russia and the United States.

Meaning: Have you ever spent the day with an acquaintance only to feel oddly deflated on the ride home? Or found yourself blindsided in the workplace by a smiling colleague delivering a scorpion-tailed remark? Scan your body to see whether you're experiencing the telltale symptoms—racing heart, flushed face, urge to strangle this person—brought on by the presence of a chum whose intentions are distinctly un-chummy. Perhaps the diagnosis will come back affirmative: Here stands a frenemy.

Used to describe a superficially amicable relationship underscored by dislike or rivalry, frenemy is an oxymoronic term. Formidable frenemies are frequent footnotes in history, from the fierce competition between celebrity scientists Thomas Edison and Nikola Tesla, to the personal slights swapped by American founding fathers (and close pals) John Adams and Thomas Jefferson. As Sigmund Freud, the founder of psychoanalysis, himself claimed: "An intimate friend and a hated enemy have always been indispensable to my emotional life." Not infrequently, Freud admitted, "friend and enemy have coincided in the same person."[1]

During its absorption into mainstream vernacular in the '90s, frenemy became inextricably associated with female friendships. The 2004 movie *Mean Girls*, which sees its protagonist navigate the brutal backstabbing of a popular female clique in high school, showcased this new, gendered iteration. As the four girls at the movie's center compete for male attention and social status, they sabotage one another with a smile.[2] An unflattering depiction rooted in sexist tropes, yes—but a study conducted by author Kelly Valen for her book, *The Twisted Sisterhood: Unraveling the Dark Legacy of Female Friendships,* found that 84% of respondents said they had suffered emotional damage at the hands of other women.

So are frenemies a female phenomenon? The formula for a frenemy—intimacy plus animosity—may crop up more frequently in female friendships, which are often built on shared confidences. Such closeness can sour. Yet the origin of the word was coined when two men—Dwight D. Eisenhower and Nikita Khrushchev—were in power. And, while high school politics can certainly get frosty, they're no match for the Cold War.

Words by Pip Usher

NOTES

1. In many ways, Freud saw fellow psychoanalyst Carl Jung as his natural successor. But after Freud twice fainted while in Jung's presence, he became suspicious and started to believe that the younger man wished him dead.
—

2. In *Mean Girls*, Lindsay Lohan's character stealthily sabotages queen bee Regina's friendships, relationships and diet. She ends up muddled as to her own intentions: "I know it may look like I was being like a bitch, but that's only because I was acting like a bitch," she insists.

Sweet Spot

The juvenile joys of the dimple.

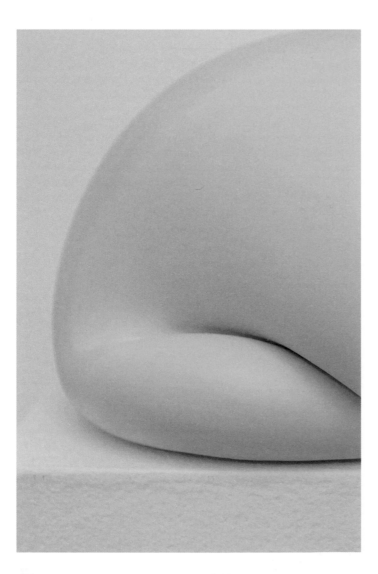

The appeal of the little dimple is simple. After all, it's also known as a gelasin, derived from the Greek word meaning "to laugh." As early as the first century, Latin poet Martial extolled its magnetic nature by deeming those without "the gelasin joyous" to have a "face less gracious." Shakespeare exalts "pretty dimpled boys, like smiling Cupids" in *Antony and Cleopatra*, and in China they are still believed to be a sign of good luck.

Most attribute the age-old allure of the dimple to its representation of youth, approachability and innocence. Almost all babies sport them in their chubby cheeks, and since we're hardwired to find newborn faces adorable, dimples elicit an almost Pavlovian tug.

The dimple, which results from a divide of the zygomaticus major muscle in the cheek, was proved to be hereditary by Gregor Mendel in the mid-1800s. But biology does not have to be destiny. According to a *New York Herald* news item, by the turn of the 20th century, surgeons had begun using a special knife to give patients overlooked by nature a "pretty, life-like dimple…as effective as the genuine print of an 'angel's kiss.'" And in 1936, American inventor Isabella Gilbert created the Dimple-Maker—a piece of headgear that pressed temporary indentations into one's face.

More recently, to meet the rising demand of a youth- and selfie-obsessed society seeking subtle ways to turn back time, surgeons have honed their skills in the field of dimpleplasty. The minimally invasive permanent procedure is a one-way ticket to looking young but not overdone.

Through generations of social and political upheaval, dimples have maintained their allure. Perpetually adorable actress Shirley Temple and her trademark dimples shot to fame during the 1930s. And things got decidedly meta when she played the title character in the 1936 film *Dimples*. Blues singer John Lee Hooker crooned, "You got dimples in your jaw… I got my eyes on you" in 1956's "Dimples." Sixty years later, BTS bemoaned the temptation of the indentation by singing "I shouldn't have seen that cheek" in 2017's "Dimple." One look at Brad Pitt or Kate Middleton, though, and you understand why they're impossible to miss.

Words by Katie Calautti

2.

Features

48 — 112

JENNY SLATE: I THINK I'M ALMOST ALWAYS ONLY TALKING ABOUT

LOVE.

What do you get when you cross a free spirit with a stand-up comedian? Over lemon squares at home in Los Angeles, *Jenny Slate* delivers the punch line. Words by *Robert Ito*, Photography by *Emman Montalvan* & Styling by *Jesse Arifien*

Jenny Slate is on stage at the Largo at the Coronet nightclub in Los Angeles, doing a very funny set. I'm furiously trying to scribble down bits of what she's saying, but the place is so dark, her set so fast and manic, that the notes come out like this: *Hippo covered with lichen. Has anyone seen my (indecipherable)? My mouth was stuffed with noodles.* Slate talks about her fiancé's beautifully crafted dreams (he's a writer) versus her own weird, intricately disturbing ones, and about how, no, you shouldn't try to "sleep it off" if you discover you've ingested poison. Dressed in a black T-shirt and black jeans, Slate is in her element, eliciting a nearly nonstop roar from fans who know her from her comedic turns on *Parks and Recreation* and *Saturday Night Live*, and likely saw her recent Netflix documentary *Stage Fright*, in which she opened up about her family, her childhood growing up in a haunted house (really), and the elusiveness of love. Three hours before this, I had been talking with Slate about some of these very things at her home, a lovely Craftsman house in nearby Silver Lake. "You're coming to my show tonight, right?" she asked. So I did.

When I first arrive at Slate's home, the front door is wide open.

Hummingbirds are flitting around in the trees. She is not dressed in a black T-shirt and black jeans, not yet, but in a long, lovely dress that has the casual look of something that you would wear while baking, sort of gingham-y. And indeed, she has been baking, lemon squares, which she offers me on a plate (delicious). Ben Shattuck, her fiancé, who is a graduate of the Iowa Writers' Workshop and a recent winner of the Pushcart Prize for best short story, comes out to say hello.

Slate shows me around, pointing out delicate treasures on her desk (rocks and seashells, a small music box) and framed photos on the walls: her mom and dad as a young couple circa the 1970s, herself—age seven—at her older sister's bat mitzvah, held aloft in a chair, eyes agog, her mouth a big, smiling "O." There are flowers everywhere, fresh cut from the garden; on one wall, there's a small framed picture of a yellow warbler that Shattuck painted for her for Christmas. "He calls me the yellow warbler," she says. In one cabinet are dozens of very tall candles of assorted colors. "I can't stop collecting candles and fabric," she says. I tell her it looks like she's preparing for some sort of ritual. "I know, it seems like we're about to do something here!" she says.

Makeup: Kirin Bhatty, Hair: Nikki Providence, Set Design: Kelly Fondry, Photo Assistants: Patrick Molina & Angel Castro

Above: Slate wears a blouse and skirt by Beaufille and shoes by Kat Maconie. Left: She wears a blouse by Beaufille and gloves by COS. Previous: She wears a sweater by COS and a coat and trousers by Aje.

Her voice drops to a near whisper. "But we're just living."

It's hard to reconcile this Jenny Slate, the one who makes lemon bars and collects candles, with the other Jenny Slate, stand-up comic. It's something she gets a lot. "I think that because I'm a comedian, people think that I'm tough," she says. "But I'm not, at all. And I'm not sarcastic. I'm just not...," she pauses, looking for the word. "I'm not *sassy*."

She is, however, busy. The foundations of Slate's career are the scene-stealing moments she created in ensemble series (*Bored to Death, Girls*) and films (2014's award-winning *Obvious Child*, in which she starred), and her celebrated voice work in animated shows, some intended for kids (*Zootopia, Star vs. the Forces of Evil*), some definitely not (*Big Mouth*).

Over the last few years, Slate has been stretching her wings with a series of acclaimed projects that have ranged far afield from many of her past endeavors. Last October, she starred in *Stage Fright*, a comedy special that combined footage from a stand-up performance at New York's Gramercy Theatre with home movies, behind-the-scenes vignettes and interviews with family members, including her two sisters (she is the middle daughter of three). In one of the most moving moments in the special, Slate talks about the often paralyzing fear she experiences before nearly every show (hence, the special's title). If just preparing to take the stage is so painful, I wonder, why do it at all? "I have stage fright right now, for tonight," she says, her body giving a shiver. "But I am of the belief that it's not asking for sympathy to be vulnerable." Besides, she says, she loves stand-up. "The second you begin," she says, "you see what's real."

Stage Fright drew rave reviews for its deep dives into everything from the joys of dressing up (*The New Yorker* described it as "a secret, gentle, creamy treat for those who love and think deeply about clothing") to the horrors of dating in the era of MeToo, when so many men are being outed as the grossest of pigs or "complicit in this ancient, heinous thing." Slate is captivating throughout, by turns flirtatious and confiding and intensely vulnerable. Indeed, her desire to be funny, she tells me, comes from "just wanting to be close to people." It also comes from a desire to push away her worries, or at least keep them at bay for a bit. "For most of my comedy," she says, "the instinct is to gather pillows of joy around myself just so I can fucking recline for a second."

A month after the release of *Stage Fright*, Slate published her first book, *Little Weirds*, a collection of personal essays that many reviewers admired (the *Washington Post* called it "eminently readable") but others struggled to define (in an otherwise adulatory review, *The New York Times* described it as "a book-shaped thing"). Slate herself described it as "small, assorted pieces of an emotional existence," but she'd rather not have to define it at all (she makes a "pffft" sound with her lips when I press her to try). Writing the book allowed her to do things, use things, she couldn't do or use in any of her other artistic outlets. "It's the privilege of being able to use everything. Use *everything*. Use all the styles that you like. Use the sad parts that, if you were going to try to put them into your stand-up comedy, might not work." Although she majored in English at Columbia, Slate never saw herself becoming a writer, so the exercise has been an unexpected joy. The book, she says, "is by far the most precious creative effort of mine yet."

Slate would like to write another book, and hopefully film another special. She also plans to start working on new material for her stand-up shows, talking "about things that are actually meaningful to me." What sorts of things? "I don't think I'll ever talk about anything but love. I think I'm almost always only talking about love."

In the meantime, she has a few films in the works. "The past nine

Left: Slate wears a blouse by Rachel Comey and her own ring. Right: She wears a dress and coat by Joseph.

Fashion is a narrative device in Slate's Netflix special, *Stage Fright*. She is filmed trying on ornate dresses belonging to her grandmother, who she credits with developing her love of dressing up. Slate recounts how Nana Connie's phone calls always come round to the same pep talk: "You're gorgeous. And it's not just that you're gorgeous. It's that you're good."

or ten months, I've taken small parts with directors I really respect," she says. Among them is a Sofia Copolla movie and she is in talks with the indie directing team The Daniels (Daniel Kwan and Daniel Scheinert). She also has a feature-length animation about her beloved character Marcel the Shell in production. In that one, she'll reprise the role she created in a series of stop-motion shorts called *Marcel the Shell with Shoes On*, in which she voices an anthropomorphic seashell whose car is a bug and whose friend is a ball of lint.

What Slate doesn't want to do anymore is work for work's sake, or continue in jobs just because she's afraid of saying she can't do them. "There are times for me when I can't act," she says. "I'm too uncomfortable. And there's something deep inside of me that does not believe in pushing through a certain type of discomfort." Rather than endure that discomfort, she says, "I guess I fail! I fail. I get fired, or I apologize and say, 'I don't think I'm good at this.' And that feels like the one thing you're not allowed to do. You're supposed to just silently hold your shame and go until exhaustion. But I really don't want to! I mean, we're all gonna die, right? I don't know why you'd wear yourself out for some shit you're bad at."

As a child, Slate often felt like she didn't quite fit: Both among her peers ("I've really always felt like I had a different personality shape than everyone else") and inside her own skin ("I can remember most of my childhood just really wanting to have an adult body"). She liked summer camp, but school was hard. "My memories of school aren't good, at all. When I think about school, the refrain is like, 'There's not enough. It's not here. I don't have the friendship that I want, I'm not being seen for myself, there isn't a place for me to be myself.'"

Perhaps that's why she'd like to help kids in similar situations, to be a mentor to someone now. "I want to be the elder or a parent or an adult who is somebody you can ask things of, and they can actually help you," she says. "I'd like to be a parent to some sort of cool person who's going to make something good." Last year, she gave a commencement address to Gwen Lynch, the sole graduating eighth grader of Cuttyhunk Elementary, a one-room schoolhouse on Cuttyhunk Island, off the coast of Cape Cod (Shattuck runs a writers' residency on the sparsely populated island). "I spent some time with Gwen, who was taller than me," Slate says. "She was confident. She pretty much knows what to do. So my speech to her was like, 'You are starting your development, you're at the beginning of your arrival into the rest of everything else. But you have the blessing of your island, your community. You have everything you need. You are mineral rich in personality and heart.'"

The sun is setting, the time coming closer to when Slate has to drive to the Largo to do her set. She is talking to me about dancing and how much she loves it, but how if she tried to dance now, everyone would laugh at her. She stops, recalling something else. She wants to tell me about something she saw recently that she'd been thinking about ever since, but she prefaces it all by saying she's probably going to regret bringing it up because it sounds like maybe she was on drugs at the time, which she definitely wasn't.

"The wind was blowing really hard from outside, and there was a curtain cord, and it was going up and down, up and down, and it was really rhythmic, and I was like, man! If I were some hotshot choreographer, I could do something at the Brooklyn Acad-emy of Music or whatever, where I make a film of this cord going up and down, up and down, and then all of a sudden the film goes off and the light comes up on stage and there's a huge replica of this night table and a huge lamp and a huge phone, and the plastic end of the cord is actually a dancer in a white leotard, and they're on a fuckin' harness and they get slammed against the wall, and you see that, and then the phone starts dancing." She's getting excited just picturing it. "And I was like, well, I'm not ever going to be able to do that, because I'm not a performance artist and I'm not a dancer, and people will just laugh at me."

"But the fact is," she continues, "I'm obsessed with that image now! And I'm happy that I could think about it. I'm happy that I could care about it."

Maybe she could write about it, I offer, in that next book of hers that she wants to write?

"Yeah, maybe I could *describe* the dance," she says. "I don't know if I have the guts to be like, hey, anyone want to do this thing with me? Or if I really want to spend nine months of my life making some kind of weird, new age ballet about a window shade cord. But I could write about it. Because I do want to write about every single thing that I've ever thought about."

"*Because I'm a comedian people think that I'm tough, but I'm not. And I'm not sarcastic.*"

Left: Slate wears a sweater by COS. Right. She wears a blouse by Beaufille and a skirt and gloves by COS.

Home Tour:
Adolf Loos

The Austrian architect laid the foundations for unornamented modernism. *Mark Baker* travels to Pilsen in the Czech Republic to see inside some of his lesser-known interiors. Photography by *Christian Møller Andersen*

The celebrated Brno-born modern architect Adolf Loos (1870–1933), who worked in the years before World War I and during the decade after, is considered a visionary for rejecting conscious ornamentation in favor of allowing a building's function to guide its design.

At the time, he was derided by many: When he designed the Looshaus on Vienna's prestigious Michaelerplatz—a building clad from the waist down in smooth marble and sporting unadorned windows set out along a simple grid—critics mocked it as having "windows without eyebrows." Habsburg Emperor Franz Joseph I, known for his highly conservative tastes, loathed it.

But Loos' daring also won him a wide swath of admirers. His buildings represented an important rejection of both the 19th-century historicist architecture so beloved by the monarchy and the then-fashionable art nouveau, which celebrated ornamentation through the ostentatious application of florid and geometric design elements. Newly wealthy industrialists, keen to show off their financial success and modern taste, flocked to commission Loos to design their houses. Both before and after the war, he designed private villas and interiors for families all around the old Austro-Hungarian Empire, in cities like Vienna, Prague and Pilsen.

The trove in Pilsen, then a booming industrial metropolis and home to the Škoda Engineering Works, was particularly rich. Loos designed at least 13 apartments and villas in the city. Eight survived the Nazi occupation and the communist period afterward and are slowly being renovated and opened to the public. The Semler apartment and Vogel apartment, both pictured here, fall at opposite ends of the spectrum: the former is still awaiting refurbishment, while the latter has now been fully restored to Loos' specifications.

In Loos' view, decorative elements, like statues and pediments, would date a building over time. For a brief period, he'd been part of the Viennese Secession art movement—the more mannered cousin of whimsical art nouveau—but a trip to the United States in the 1890s had opened his eyes to a competing vision for modern architecture. He admired the dazzling skyscrapers from architects such as Louis Sullivan, with their emphasis on utility, and eventually channeled their influence into *Ornamentation and Crime*, his 1910 lecture that later became a key text in architectural theory. Ornamentation, Loos believed, should flow from the intrinsic, timeless qualities of the materials used, through distinctive elements like the veining in a slab of marble or the hue or grain of a panel of wood.

Although Loos was dismissive of the need for ornamentation, he used rich materials to finish his interiors including polished wood and stone paneling.

The Vogel apartment was built according to Loos' concept of Raumplan—a way of designing that imagined an interior as "contiguous, continual spaces."

It's the aura and beauty of those precious materials that still strike visitors today on entering the Semler apartment, built in 1931 for Helena and Hugo Semler. The apartment is awaiting renovation—only the dining, living and "lady's" rooms have survived. But the rich marble cladding on some walls, particularly its elaborate veining, and the high quality of the wood paneling and built-in wooden fixtures still exude a calming effect. In the lady's room, a yellowish elm imparts a playful feel, while in the dining and living rooms, a darker and more intricately grained walnut lends an impression of opulence.

Petr Domanický, a curator for the West Bohemian Gallery in Pilsen and an expert on Loos, says Loos' unique talent was his "extraordinary spatial imagination." Open-plan living concepts were rare at the time, but Loos introduced sliding door panels into the space. "The apartment's characteristic features are the connection of the living and dining rooms, the axial symmetry of the space, and its accentuation with pillars, fireplaces and dining tables in the intersection of the axes," Domanický says.

The second Pilsen apartment, built for Dr. Josef Vogel and his wife, Štěpánka, in 1928, presents a different first impression. Unlike the derelict Semler apartment, the Vogel interior has been painstakingly restored to look exactly as it did when it was built. It is notably brighter, with yellowish travertine on the walls of the dining room, and redder, warmer cherry wood in place of walnut.

Domanický says, though, that both apartments share many of the same virtues. "The Vogel apartment impresses mainly by how the rooms open up to each other and with its axial symmetry, marked end-to-end with distinctive motifs, like a fireplace and mirrors." For visitors, the real joy comes through seeing how Loos used interior furnishings to accent his architectural designs. In fact, Loos created many of his own furniture pieces and accessories. Most notable among these in the Vogel apartment are the spherical hanging lamp in the dining room, a long wall-unit sofa, an Arts and Crafts-inspired fireplace grill, and reproductions of several Loos-designed chairs. These include his signature "Knieschwimmer" lounger, looking something like an upholstered hammock, where the sitter feels suspended in space.

When the German army occupied Czechoslovakia, and Pilsen, at the start of World War II, the Semlers—a Jewish family—fled their prestigious apartment before the Nazis seized it to use as their army headquarters. In the final days of the war, on May 6, 1945, the US Army, advancing from the west, captured Pilsen. The town erupted in joy at the liberation and German soldiers deserted in droves.

The Americans entered the Semler apartment and demanded that the presiding German officer, Lt. Gen. Georg von Majewski, issue an unconditional surrender. There, at his desk in the living room, in the presence of his wife, staff and the American officers, Majewski duly signed the capitulation order.

Then, in a moment that might have been scripted in Hollywood, Majewski pulled out a service revolver that he'd hidden from view. He turned the gun to his body, pulled the trigger and slumped over in a pool of blood.

Even today, if you listen carefully, it's almost as if you can still hear the sounds of the blast echoing off those refined marbled walls.

"Ornamentation, Loos believed, should flow from the intrinsic, timeless qualities of the materials used, through distinctive elements like the veining in a slab of marble."

The marbled room at the Semler apartment was used as a music salon.

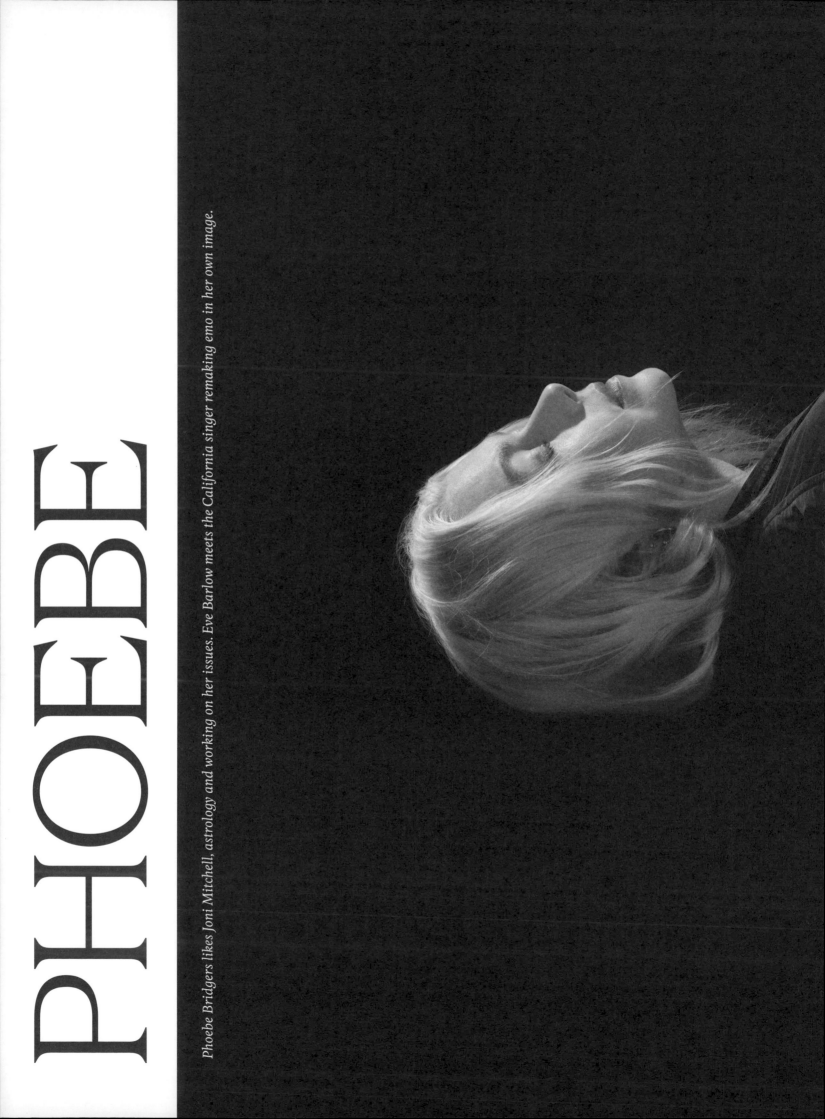

PHOEBE

Phoebe Bridgers likes Joni Mitchell, astrology and working on her issues. Eve Barlow meets the California singer remaking emo in her own image.

67

Photography by Emman Montalvan & Styling by Jesse Arifien

Left: Bridgers wears a shirt by COS. Previous: She wears a trench coat by Jac + Jack.

"All I ever do on tour is save recipes on my phone."

On February 29, 2016, Phoebe Bridgers made a list of goals she wanted to achieve by the next leap year. They included: tour the world, see Ireland, make three albums. She'd never left the US. She'd never made a record. She was 21 and unsigned. Now she's 25. She's toured the world, including Ireland, and released three albums: one solo, one as boygenius with Lucy Dacus and Julien Baker, and one as Better Oblivion Community Center with Conor Oberst—her hero.

"Dude!" she says, of revisiting the list on February 29, 2020. "It's happened. They all became real in ways I couldn't have imagined." It's mid-morning in LA, and Bridgers is calling while doing a lap of the local Silver Lake Reservoir. She's California born and bred. She "ums" with every response, employs "later" for goodbye and admits to spending "$11 on smoothies on average per day." She talks up astrology: She blames Mercury being in retrograde for feeling sick during a press week in New York City. "I was convinced I had coronavirus," she says. She played Carnegie Hall and her manager stood on the side of the stage with a box of tissues. Bridgers was promoting her second solo album, *Punisher*, made over the past year with Tony Berg and Ethan Gruska, the producers who worked on her debut, *Stranger in the Alps*. Although this time Bridgers donned a producer's hat, too.

Talking about the album has meant wrapping her head around her personal songs. "I don't know what I'm thinking when I'm writing. It's meta—it just happens," she says. "The perspective doesn't come for years. I can write a crazy fucked-up emotional lyric, then I'm onstage singing it for the 80th time in a row and I see someone singing the lyric and think, 'Oh my God! I know what that's about now.'"

It was back in 2017 that Bridgers was dubbed a leading lyricist of her generation. *Stranger in the Alps* set her up for late-night TV, critical praise and a tour that lasted far too long. "All I ever do on tour is save recipes on my phone," she offers. "I fantasize about being at home." Her final stint in 2019 with Better Oblivion Community Center was exhausting. "I was on tour with my best friends, in a

Hair and Makeup: Nicole Wittman using MAC Cosmetics

Left: Bridgers wears a suit by COS and her own shoes. Overleaf: She wears a shirt by COS and earrings by Broken English.

"Songs are proof that I'm getting progressively better over my life."

van with one of my heroes, crushing shows. But when the show was over, I would get in my bunk and stare into darkness. I needed a break, you know?"

The music she wrote in the wake of that was reactive. There was a crash, and a depression. Bridgers says she dissociated—she would find herself writing lyrics almost absentmindedly, not realizing their meaning until later. She was adjusting to normality after her dreams came true. "Making this record was a breath of fresh air: going to sleep in the same bed, waking up in the same place," she says. "I've grown up a lot." The songs she wrote are a catalog of her early 20s. "I make so many resolutions, so many plans. Songs are proof that I'm getting progressively better over my life."

Punisher is an album about rootlessness, homesickness, solitude. She doesn't paint herself favorably or hold back from inflicting hurt ("*I hate your mom / I hate it when she opens her mouth*," is one of the harshest lines). "I can't lie in my music," she says. "Every time when I've thought, 'I should blur the lines. That might hurt somebody's feelings,' I can't do it." Songs are Bridgers' way of understanding her patterns, of holding herself accountable. For example, she explains why she prefers fixing others—in both romance and friendship—at the expense of fixing herself: "It's intoxicating; if I'm the one arguing for light and love, I don't have to be the dark one. If

someone's more positive than me then I don't know how to deal with that."

Bridgers grew up in Pasadena, just north of LA, listening to the family's vinyl collection: Joni Mitchell, Hank Williams, The Pretenders. Her family wasn't as wealthy as those of her schoolfriends. "I didn't grow up with money at all," says Bridgers. "My friends' parents were directors. They would have organic-y food in their lunches. It made me feel like shit," she says. For high school, Bridgers decided to go to the Los Angeles County High School for the Arts, LACHSA, a publicly funded performing arts school whose alumni include HAIM, Zoey Deutch and Josh Groban. There she joined punk band Sloppy Jane, fronted by her best friend, Haley Dahl. "The cool kids at LACHSA were cooler than any other kids. There were different scenes: dancers, people who wore fucking clown makeup every day. I don't know if I fit with any of them," she says.

Sloppy Jane set Bridgers up. When the band was invited to star in an iPhone commercial in 2014, Dahl was against it, so Bridgers stepped in as frontwoman. She funded her first foray into record-making with the earnings. "I didn't have a job—it was right out of high school. I kinda signed myself." At home, Bridgers' mother was her champion. She drove her through the night ("So I could play in fucking Riverside") to build her

reputation. She took her to shows. Her first was Neil Young at Staples Center: "Rad." Bridgers' parents remained together until she was 19. She's alluded to her father being abusive and having drug problems. On her new song "Kyoto" she seems to address him: "*You called me from a payphone... To tell me you're getting sober and you wrote me a letter / But I don't have to read it.*" "Everybody deals with addiction and fucking weird family dynamics," she says. "It speaks to that." For all of Bridgers' earnestness, her online persona is humor-centric. Her Twitter name is a play on the grocery chain Trader Joe's (Traitor Joe) and her Instagram handle is @_fake_nudes_. She almost shares a name with another leading woman in the zeitgeist: *Fleabag* creator Phoebe Waller-Bridge. "I want to marry her," she says. "We would end up with the same name if we hyphenated it." Phoebe Bridgers-Waller-Bridge has a good ring to it. Bridgers says she is relieved to be confused with someone she's a fan of. "Imagine if it was a contestant on *The Bachelor* and I was having to deal with that every day."

Bridgers is in constant demand as a collaborator. Her backing vocals appear on the forthcoming album from The 1975, and she's supporting them on tour. "It's gonna be like summer camp," she says. She's also on Perfume Genius' forthcoming album. Her own LP is an embarrassment of riches featuring Jenny Lee Lindberg

of Warpaint, Lucy Dacus, Julien Baker, Grammy Award-winning producer Blake Mills and Oberst. (After listening through her record, he called her with his review: "Crazy.")

Her album is named after the millennial slang term "punisher": someone who talks too much. Bridgers offers an example: "Your aunt has a new boyfriend. It's Thanksgiving. He's talking about how he switched from Verizon to AT&T for a half hour. You're the direct person he's talking to. You're being punished. He's a punisher." Has there been a moment when she thought she might have been a punisher? "Maybe with Joni Mitchell," she says. "I may or may not have punished Joni Mitchell." Bridgers met Mitchell at a Mavis Staples concert in LA. "There's nothing I can say to this woman that hasn't been said four trillion times. Joni Mitchell doesn't need to hear anybody say that she changed their life. Ever again."

As Bridgers gets ready to embark upon a new journey, has she made a list for the next leap year: 2024? "I did!" she says. It's more esoteric. "I want meaningful friendships. I want to love my therapist." She laughs. Bridgers has a therapist, but they haven't clicked yet. "I wanna be one of those people who's like: I *love* my therapist." As she puts in the time and does the work, it will be a result that says more about Bridgers than it does the therapist.

Above: Bridgers wears a dress by Perfect Number and slides by Bassike. Right: She wears a denim jacket and jeans by AJE.

It's the little things that count—and that drive us to distraction. Photography by Aaron Tilley ⊘ Styling by Sandy Suffield

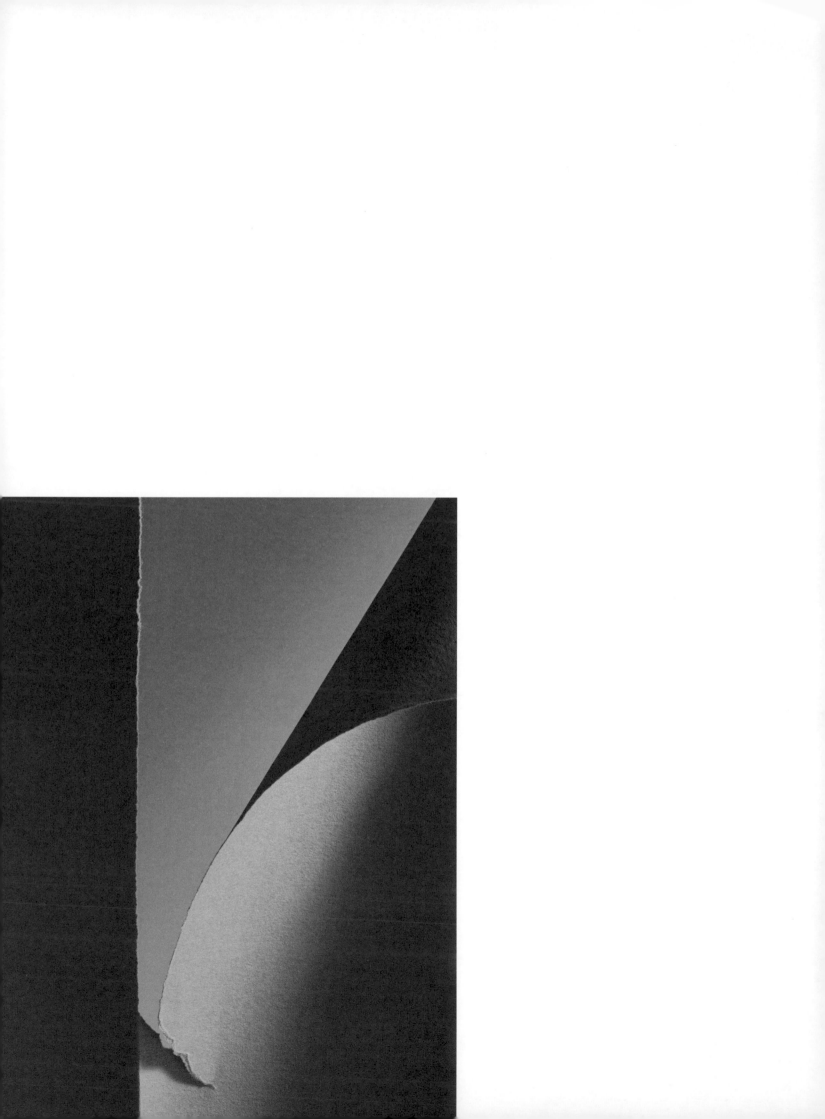

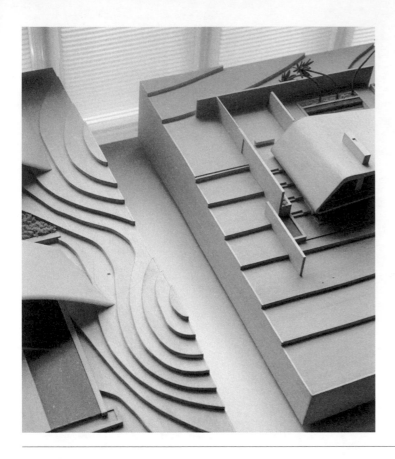

At Work With:
Hariri & Hariri

From the Iranian desert to the New York architecture studio they co-founded, sisters *Gisue Hariri* and *Mojgan Hariri* have always been "partners in crime." *Charles Shafaieh* meets them in Manhattan. Photography by *Claire Cottrell*

FEATURES

When sisters Gisue Hariri and Mojgan Hariri began studying architecture at Cornell University in the 1970s, they were unaware of the opposition they would encounter as women in the field. Born in Iran in 1956 and 1958 respectively, they grew up in the desert—where their father worked as an engineer on the oil fields—and had no preconceptions of who architects could be or what the work entailed. Still, the unknown did not deter them. For over three decades now, the Hariris have run an internationally renowned studio in New York City, where they are celebrated for a holistic approach that puts as much emphasis on the furniture and smallest accessories as on a design's grand structure. Whether in Salzburg or Tehran, they are inspired by Iranian culture's reverence for nature as well as by its poetry.

The Hariris continue to challenge dominant ideologies in architecture. Rather than focus on high-profile commissions or even paychecks, they are working independently on an alternative solution to refugee housing: and emerging transient communities. Scheduled to exhibit at the Venice Architecture Biennale, their innovative prototype—"a foldable pod for disaster relief"—asks whether it's possible to design a generic shelter that would be practical and affordable for the homeless worldwide.

CS: *What stands out from your experience as women entering the male-dominated School of Architecture at Cornell in the 1970s?* **MH:** It wasn't a case of a male versus female view. There was only one way to see the world: the man's way. **GH:** Iran is a very segregated universe, and the struggle was always between men and women. We went to segregated schools; everywhere you felt you had to protect yourself because the men were freer. Even in the physicality of residential neighborhoods where homes had tall walls around them, you saw, from an early age, women as more in the interior and that public [space] was for men. Coming to America, my expectations were from Hollywood movies: big universities, freedom, equality. Entering a very small college that was unaccepting of women and having to be on your own was difficult and eye-opening. We were very secluded and had to protect each other. **MH:** The difference between the genders was shocking, too. We thought American women would be strong and liberated but found it completely otherwise. **GH:** In a way, we had to become their nurturers and protectors! In Iran, there was backstabbing and competition amongst the women, of course, but it was like sibling rivalry. We looked after each other to create a group so no one could push us around.

CS: *Why did you decide to set up your studio together?* **MH:** Architecture is a creative and competitive process with lots of emotion. I trusted Gisue and knew if she opposed something I was drawing, it wasn't egotistical. If we criticized one another, it was to push the project further, not stop the other. Being sisters, we knew that wouldn't happen. **GH:** When you enter the profession, you realize that, unlike at school where one architect does their own project and hides everything, in offices a group

Gisue Hariri (pictured left) has spoken about the need for an architect's fashion sense to reflect their design style—in her case that means clothes that are "sculptural, dynamic, and structured."

works together; everyone pulls, pushes, erases and complements to make a project become concrete. Yes, the designer is kind of the creative link, but design is only a small part of it. The School of Architecture didn't teach us this! When the awakening came, it was obvious to me that Mojgan and I could make a team. We grew up together and learned we could look at something and communicate in a kind of language, if you will, that didn't require talking. We were not afraid; there were two of us—we could stay up longer together. It's a tight-knit collaboration that makes our projects not twice as good but 10 times better.

CS: *You literally dug through the earth together growing up in the desert. How did that landscape influence you?* **MH:** [How] your environment changes your outlook will always be with you. For example, I get claustrophobic in woodsy areas. I want to see the horizon wherever I go! The desert is boundless. There is so much contrast—just blue and the color of earth, coming together in one line. It's so abstract and beautiful, like a blank canvas on which you can do whatever you want. **GH:** What was fascinating was there was nothing besides the desert. No green parks, public spaces, museums, toys. **MH:** It had snakes and lizards. **GH:** And we played with them! All that was given to you was this vastness. And you need to have a comrade. **MH:** A comrade in crime. **GH:** To discover. It was about going out and entertaining ourselves. In that sense, it was very nurturing and important because today we're bombarded by so much information that there isn't time to think. I want to take students someplace with no people or internet so they can go inside themselves and just think for a bit. We were lucky we had that time, and one another, to talk, ask questions and discover things. Now we have a love for rocks and their shapes, and a passion for space, blankness and vastness.

CS: *Mojgan has used the metaphor of architecture being a "long-distance marathon." Do you see time as essential to understanding a work?* **GH:** For me, architecture is always about experience; it's about space and light, and their articulation. That they are intangible brings in metaphysics, philosophy… quantum mechanics! We've considered whether [we think about this] because we're Persian: Sufi poets talk about "everything and nothing." All these philosophical quests relate to architecture, but no one tells you how to articulate experience. It's something internal. You have to know who human beings are and what "nothing and everything" means. It doesn't have a formula. **MH:** We know we've done something good when our clients' habits and behavior change after a project finishes. That experience allows them to make themselves better.

CS: *Your emphasis on socially responsible architecture, such as your refugee pod, signals that architecture's capacity to improve lives should not be restricted to the 1% and their luxury apartments.* **MH:** The word luxury has become meaningless. **GH:** One has to redefine it—perhaps as affordable or in good taste, locally made, sustainable. **MH:** In New York, a housing project and a luxury building have the exact same structure. So why should we even have luxury buildings? You can make things out of gold that nobody needs or wants, but essentially, it's the same materials. There's no reason why good materials and standards of living shouldn't be applied to affordable housing.

CS: *What is the path forward?* **GH:** Private developers and governments need to come together. Companies like Amazon and Google that go where they think space and housing are available need to work with great architects to create innovative, affordable ideas. **MH:** Unfortunately, with our environmental situation, until everybody comes together there will be no solutions. We are just destroying the earth.

CS: *Will architecture in the future be identical to today's, or is architecture undefinable because it is always evolving?* **MH:** If architecture doesn't evolve with technology, people's mindsets and available materials, it dies. **GH:** Architecture, like life, is paradoxical in the sense that matter and energy are never created or destroyed; they constantly transform into one thing or another. It's not about style—it's about vision.

"We could communicate in a language that didn't require talking."

Essay:

The Vacant Muse

Words by Rebecca Liu

In Ancient Greece, the nine Muses were goddesses who inspired artists to complete their work. Today, the figure of the muse is still shrouded in an other-worldly aura: from Dora Maar to Margot Robbie, the women who "inspire" artists are often treated as blank canvases primed to channel the creativity of others. Rebecca Liu goes behind the scenes at the studio.

In Ottessa Moshfegh's recent hit novel *My Year of Rest and Relaxation*, the unnamed protagonist, a beautiful blonde misanthrope living in New York, induces a drug-filled hibernation that lasts four months. Her mission is supported by Ping Xi, a rising artist and longtime admirer, who periodically brings food and supplies to her apartment. In return, the protagonist allows him to make art about her. "The creative incentive for me is that you'll be constantly... naive," he tells her. While she sleeps, she imagines Xi's paintings: "They were all 'sleeping nudes,' mussed beds and tangles of pale limbs and blond hair."

Many common metaphors about the artist's muse are made literal in this story. The artist's inspiration—young, gorgeous, female—is tranquilized; she's an object on which others project their fantasies. The artist—male, authoritative, voyeuristic—captures her essence, translating what is seen as ineffable about a woman's personal spirit into public display. "For too many centuries women have been busy being muses," Anaïs Nin wrote in her 1976 essay, "The New Woman": "In the letters I've received from women, I've found... a guilt for creating. It's a very strange illness, and it doesn't strike men—because the culture has demanded of man that he give his maximum talents."

Look to the origins of the muse in Greek mythology, and its gendered dimensions are hard to ignore. The original Muses were the nine daughters of Zeus and Mnemosyne, the goddess of memory. As ancient deities of song, dance and memory, the nine Muses gave artists the inspiration needed to complete their work. Writers such Hesiod and Homer called upon them for guidance. In the opening lines of *The Odyssey*, Homer says, "Sing in me, Muse, and through me tell the story of that man skilled in all ways of contending, the wanderer, harried for years on end."

The notion of the artist's muse has been carried down from the Greeks to the modern day. But now muses are more often associated with mortal women, rather than mythic gods. Pablo Picasso was famously inspired by his partners: The most recognized of his muses, Marie-Thérèse Walter, became the mistress of the artist, then 45, when she was 17. Walter was cheerful and athletic in real life, her granddaughter recounted in an interview with *Artsy*: "Curiously, such attributes depart from the usual image of Marie-Thérèse as she appears in Picasso's paintings: as a reclining or, most often, sleeping muse." The active, exciting lives of his muses were erased on the canvas, rendered passive by the artist's brush. Other Picasso muses were artists in their own right, including surrealist photographer Dora Maar (also model to photographer May Ray) and Françoise Gilot, who wrote about her difficult relationship with the often abusive painter in her 1990 memoir, *Life With Picasso*.[1] In it, she remembers, "He was rather fond, also, of saying, 'For me there are only two kinds of women: goddesses and doormats.'" Elsewhere, he told her, "Women are machines for suffering."

Picasso was not alone in associating inspiration with a tortured, passive form of womanhood. Andy Warhol said of his muse, American actress Edie Sedgwick, that "she had more problems than anyone I'd ever met," describing her as having "a poignantly vacant, vulnerable quality... She was a wonderful, beautiful blank." Sometimes it is not suffering, but rather the naive, empty goodness of muses that inspires artists. Responding to recent criticisms of Margot Robbie's lack of dialogue in his latest film, *Once Upon a Time in Hollywood*, director Quentin Tarantino said that Robbie's character, Sharon Tate, "is an angelic presence throughout the movie... to some degree, she's not in the movie, she's in our hearts."

These famous cases all involve a female muse inspiring a male artist. There are notable exceptions: French painter Berthe Morisot was inspired by her husband, Eugène Manet, and "mutual muse" couples exist: Frida Kahlo and Diego Rivera, and Georgia O'Keeffe and Alfred Stieglitz among them.[2] But the power dynamics associated with the muse as it is popularly understood—a vehicle for someone else's creativity—feel inextricable from traditional gender inequalities that subordinate women to the creativity of men. In this schema, women are rewarded not so much for being well-rounded voices unto themselves, but resplendent vehicles for those of others.

"The central issue with the concept of the muse is that it mystifies the actual social conditions of art-making, the dynamics of power and privilege in it," says Allison Deutsch, Leverhulme Early Career Fellow in the Department of History of Art at Birkbeck, University of London. "This slippage between muse as allegorical figure, and muse as living model, creates all sorts of problems. It collapses a complex relationship between two people, both engaged in forms of labor, into the stuff of mystery and fantasy, pleasure and peril—where nobody is really working." These very questions of who gets to make work and who is merely seen to inspire it has emerged in a recent controversy concerning the Japanese model Kaori, former muse and collaborator to prolific photographer Nobuyoshi Araki. In a blog post published two years ago, Kaori spoke of the bullying and exploitation she experienced in their relationship—but also crucially took issue with what she saw as her erasure in the photographer's legacy. "In the world of art, the lives of muses are mythologized and made into beautiful and tragic tales," she writes. Being a muse to one of the nation's most famous artists, however, brought her little economic or social power. "After being a model for 16 years, I had built nothing. I had nothing," she says.

NOTES

1. In her memoir, Gilot writes about how she consented to live her life with Picasso on his terms. "At the time I went to live with Pablo, I had felt that he was a person to whom I could, and should, devote myself entirely, but from whom I should expect to receive nothing beyond what he had given the world by means of his art," she writes.

2. Kahlo's image has become iconic—reproduced everywhere from nail decals to socks in a phenomenon that has been termed "Fridamania." Her popularity is partly motivated by the belief that she refused to subjugate herself to the male gaze. It's telling that a quote from the artist Oroma Elewa—"I am my own muse. I am the subject I know best. The subject I want to know better," is frequently misattributed to Kahlo.

"Could we approach the objects of artists' inspirations not as voiceless, mythic essences, but as rich collaborators in their own right?"

American poet and author Kelley Swain worked as an artist's model across the US and Europe for 10 years, and reflected on her experiences in her 2016 memoir, *The Naked Muse*. For Swain, being an artist's model had little to do with the glossy, mythic tragedy often attached to the muse. It was, rather, work. "I kind of just fell into modelling," she remembers, "because a friend who was doing it for an art class needed a substitute. It was very interesting to me because I had always wanted to study a bit more about art… so I was getting paid to sit in on art classes, basically."

Rather than feeling like these artists were "translating" her spirit, Swain could see paintings about her from a cooler distance: "That's not *you*, but it's you as captured by someone." Her personal experiences have been overwhelmingly positive, and this sense of equality between artist and model means that it was "fun," rather than stressful, "to be depicted as different characters." For Swain, modeling has taught her something about herself, too: "It was a wonderful intellectual exercise for me… I'm so often in my head and it helped me to be more in my body."

Swain's positive experiences as a model, and as someone who learns and grows alongside artists, points to a new way of making art, one based on mutual respect and equality. Could we approach the objects of artists' inspirations not as voiceless, mythic essences, but as rich collaborators in their own right? Though the legends associated with the muse might indulge our romantic fantasies, it is worth asking what critical questions get lost in our drive to mythologize the artistic labor between two people. "We often talk of artists being inspired," notes Deutsch, "but this, too, is vague and mysterious, and it elides matters of agency. Inspiration, even if it is tied to a so-called muse, seems also to come from nowhere. Instead, we might think about an artist's sources or an artist's influences." Let the sleeping muse awaken, and from her renewed agency, our own approaches to the labor of art be a bit more enlightened.

ISLAND TIME

Stretching out the summer on Madeira's volcanic coastline. Photography by Romain Laprade & Styling by Camille-Joséphine Teisseire

Right: Marsella wears a blouse by Tatiane de Freitas as a headscarf and a swimsuit by Voiment Intimates. Overleaf: Marsella wears a swimsuit by Talia Collins.

Hair & Makeup: Ana Raquel Ribeiro

The German conceptual artist Rebecca Horn has spent a half-century using fans, feathers and curious masks to extend the

REBECCA

Photography: Mechanical Body Fan, 1972-1974. Courtesy of Rebecca Horn / VG Bild Kunst / VISDA

human body—and comment on its fragility. Words by Cody Delistraty

107

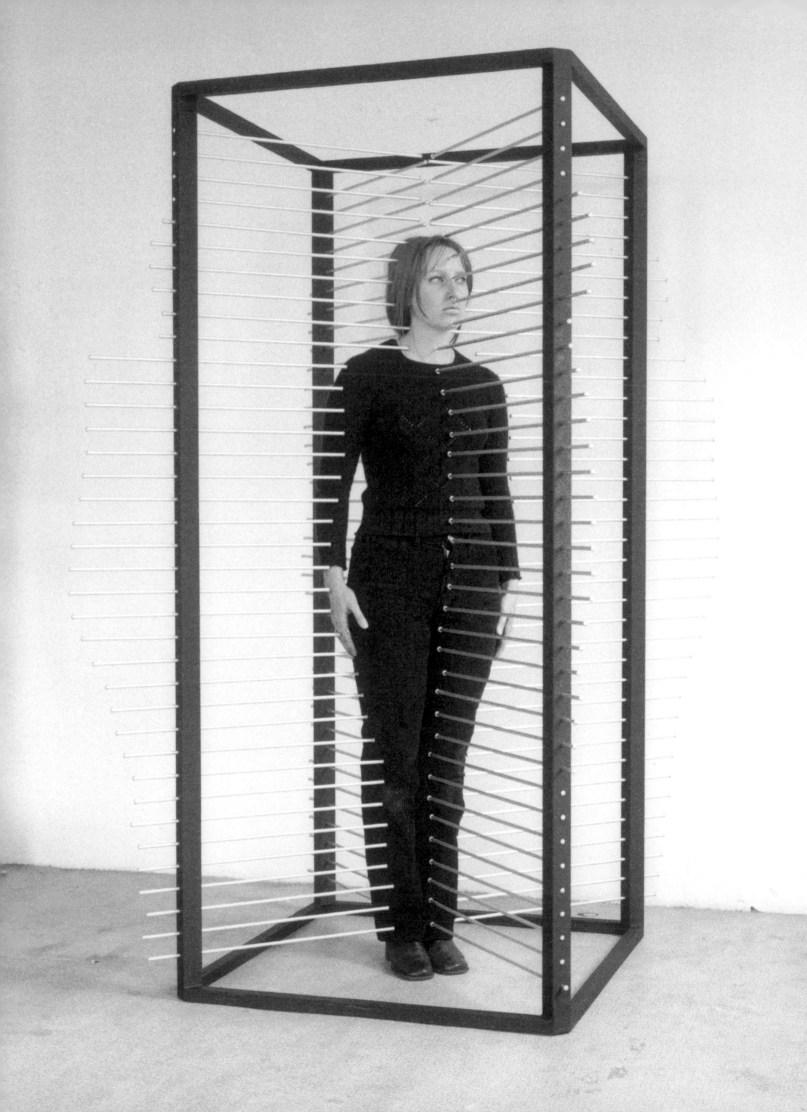

Left Photograph: Measure Box, 1970. Courtesy of Rebecca Horn / VG Bild Kunst / VISDA. Right Photograph: Chris Felver/Getty Images

In 1964, while living in Barcelona and staying in a hotel where the rooms were rented by the hour, Rebecca Horn began her artistic career. She was 20 and had just enrolled in the Hamburg Academy of Fine Arts but had been forced to drop out: Over the next few years, she would become increasingly and inexplicably physically weak. After her parents both died, she started to feel isolated as well. By 1967, says Alexandra Müller, a curator at the Centre Pompidou-Metz, which recently mounted an exhibition of Horn's work, Horn had certainly contracted lung poisoning from the toxic fumes she'd been breathing while sculpting polyester resins without a mask. She was committed to a year in a sanatorium to recover—an "unbearable" experience for her, Müller says.

The body—its limitations, its fallibility, its capacity for debilitating sickness and death—became the center of Horn's burgeoning artistic practice. In the sanatorium, she began to create her first "body sculptures." Growing up in post–World War II Bavaria, she had been taught to draw by her Romanian governess. She rarely spoke as a girl, and almost never spoke German if she did. "Germans were hated. We had to learn French and English. We were always traveling somewhere else, speaking something else," Horn said in a rare 2005 interview with *The Guardian*. "I did not have to draw in German or French or English. I could just draw."

At the sanatorium, she returned to the drawing of her childhood, conceiving of mythical, physically impossible humans, blessed and burdened with additional appendages. Perhaps her most famous artwork, "Einhorn" (1970), is both a work of performance and a physical work of art. A "sculptural garment," "Einhorn," meaning unicorn, is a single white horn strapped around the wearer's head. It looks similar to the body straps depicted in Frida Kahlo's "Broken Column" (1944), which Kahlo was forced to use to stabilize her spine after a near-fatal tram crash. "Einhorn" is violent, but it is also a reference to art history, and even funny—a play on words with the artist's own name.

Violence began to appear everywhere in Horn's work. In her 20s and 30s, it emerged in her reinventions of the physical body. Horn's "Hahnenmaske" (1973), or Cockfeather Mask, is made of a fabric-covered strip of metal and black feathers that bends to the wearer's face, stroking anyone who comes near. Like a number of her works, it looks like a sadomasochist device. "Federkleid" (1972), Feather Dress, is a set of feathers that covers a naked man and is held together by strings. Horn can pull and release to raise the feathers up or down, giving her the power to expose or protect the man's nakedness. But perhaps there is no more disturbing work than her video installation "Buster's Bedroom," in which a hospital patient who's pretending to be a doctor—played improbably by a young Donald Sutherland—puts a straightjacket onto a young woman. A real straightjacket, displayed in the gallery next to the screen, inflates and deflates itself as the girl in the video shouts "That hurts!"

"Buster's Bedroom"—and much of Horn's early oeuvre—implies that not only might we have power over our bodies taken away, but that our lack of power might become a source of entertainment for another. The effect of these works is a greater realization of one's own body and ability but also its fickleness. With sufficient training, for instance, one might run a marathon, but also, with a well-placed slice to our Achilles tendon, never walk again. The line between good and evil, life and death, movement and incapacitation is outlandishly thin, to the degree that to believe one has control over anything, even one's own flesh and bones, is a dangerously arrogant assumption. Horn's art forces one to watch another's pain and bodily incapacitation.

It's not a coincidence that many of the 20th-century artists who grappled the most with the pain of others are German. In the mid-1970s, Horn moved to New York, where she lived for a decade before she returned to Germany and began to wrestle with her home country's historical legacy, evolving her art from the individual body to the wider society. She created "Concert in Reverse" (1987), a sound work that she installed at the site of Nazi torture and executions, which recreated the sounds of struggling, dying prisoners. Horn also reopened a

tower that Nazis had used to torture prisoners and added in steel hammers and flickering lights to create a site of memory that cannot be changed.

For Horn, the body is history and history is the body. "Horn's work [is a testament to] her consciousness of the world where brutality and pain are inseparable from a dramatic tension," says Müller. For most people, the response to our inability to change our past, and, in many ways, to even change anything about our future, is to pretend we have more agency than we do—to claim control even where we do not have it. But for others, as Horn's art shows, the solution to having no existential control is to enact violence and pain as one can—to assert control at any cost.

It is often the great challenge of enterprising performance artists—from Horn to the late Ulay—to archive and maintain the relevance of their works. So contingent on their immediate context, Horn's pieces are either impossible to recreate elsewhere or simply become irrelevant in other contexts. Even a physical piece like "Pencil Mask," a body extension artwork with nine leather straps that looks like an S&M hood but actually allows the wearer to use her face to draw, requires a knowledgeable wearer. It is not like a painting; it cannot be easily, or at least passively, "read" in a gallery setting.

As early as her 20s, Horn anticipated this challenge and hired photographers to memorialize her performances, most frequently the photographer Achim Thode.

Her intention to make her fleeting works permanent, Müller says, changed how she performed. Each performance was effectively being done twice: first the performance for the audience, then the performance for the photographer. "The artist becomes, like Yves Klein, Joseph Beuys, or others before, the producer of his own myth," says Müller. "Rebecca Horn has ensured, or rather directed, the visual immortality of her ephemeral works."

Horn diversified the modes of consumption for a number of her artworks in order to give them historical longevity, says Sandra Beate Reimann, a curator at the Museum Tinguely, in Basel, which recently presented a Horn retrospective. Reimann cites "White Body Fan" (1972), which Horn has performed, and had filmed and photographed. She also lets museums and galleries borrow the object at the center of the piece—a contraption that encases the wearer in an enormous white fan made of metal and wood.

Though Horn has been working for the better part of 60 years, today, at 76 years old, she is still relatively unknown. A shame. Her art captures the beauty of physical movement as well as any of the thematically similar but more popular contemporary artists like Yvonne Rainer, Vito Acconci or Bruce Nauman. Yet Horn singularly prioritizes the investigation of psychological movement as well. "You have to believe in something, and you have to give that out to the world," Horn says. "Most people live in a little prison in their minds."

"Einhorn" (pictured right) was a performance in which a woman walked through the countryside for 12 hours with a unicorn-like horn attached to her head.

"You have to believe in something, and you have to give that out to the world. Most people live in a little prison in their minds."

3.

Movement

---

114 — 176

MARION MOTIN:

I WANT TO SEE *HUMANS* ON STAGE, NOT DANCERS.

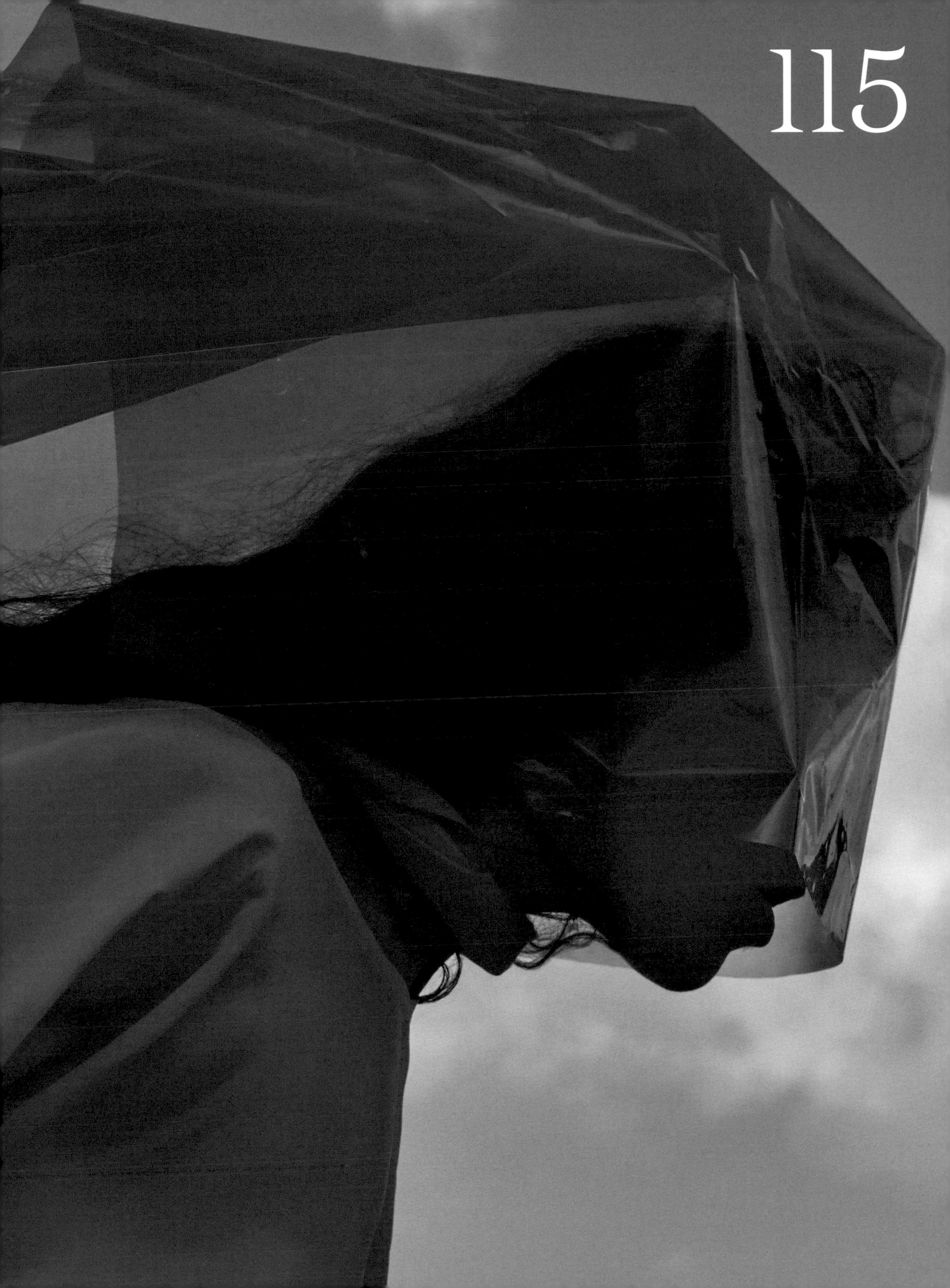

Above: Motin wears a top, trousers, sweater and dress by Baserange. Previous: She wears a dress by Nehera.

In the 1990s, *Marion Motin* swapped ballet classes for hip-hop battlegrounds in the Parisian banlieues. The celebrated choreographer talks to *Daphnée Denis* about her guiding belief in "immediate movement"—and why touring with Madonna almost broke her. Photography by *Cédric Viollet* & Styling by *Mélodie Zagury*

Hair & Makeup: Gaëlle Bonnot, Producer: Ségolène Legrand, Photo Assistant: Victor Gueret, Agent: Clara Hautecoeur

When she was a child, Marion Motin would lie on the vacuum cleaner while it was on to feel it vibrating. "My mother used to tell me that I was very receptive to all the weird music of daily life—I would even shake my head to the sound of the dog eating out of its bowl," she recalls. In the years since, the 39-year-old contemporary dancer and choreographer has made a career out of seeking what makes her vibrate: finding moves that feel right rather than rehearsed. She calls this "the immediate movement," something so deeply ingrained in her being that she needs to act it out in order to describe it.

"It's an instinctive movement, one you want to do right now, not just something you execute without knowing why. No, it's like, right now I want to do *this*. Aargh!" she says with a growl, her body shaken by an invisible pull. "You have to feel it inside, it really comes from within somehow, and it's… it's real." Though her busy schedule doesn't allow for a face-to-face, she has agreed to the next best thing—FaceTime—aware that I might want to *watch* her answers as well as listen to them. "Yes, I'm very expressive," she concedes.

As a performer, Motin has joined Madonna on tour, appeared on music videos for Robbie Williams and Jamiroquai, and danced for choreographers including Angelin Preljoçaj and Sylvain Groud. As a choreographer, she is best known in the English-speaking world for her collaboration with Christine and the Queens (the stage name of singer Héloïse Adelaïde Letissier), whose Chaleur Humaine tour she choreographed, as well as for her work on Dua Lipa's "IDGAF" music video, which was nominated for best choreography at the 2018 MTV Video Music Awards. Her show *Rouge*, commissioned by Rambert, London's legendary contemporary dance company, has been received with acclaim.[1] She currently splits her time between choreographing the tour of Belgian pop sensation Angèle, working as an advisor on film sets, and preparing a show with her own dance company as an artist-in-residence at the theater in her native Saint-Lô, in Normandy. Working with both untrained and professional dancers doesn't faze her. "I want to see humans on stage, not dancers," she says. "Dance bores me, actually."

Motin's relationship to dancing has always been ambivalent. Growing up, she and her sister took ballet classes, but the rigidity of the classical training rapidly got on her nerves. She much preferred imitating

NOTES

1. Motin's commission to choreograph for Rambert was a particularly profound accomplishment, because the company rarely works with so-called "commercial" choreographers. *Rouge* is a group piece devised largely through improvisation that explores how we regenerate energy when physically "in the red."
—

2. In the 1990s, hip-hop grew influential in France. In 1997, the Marseille-based group IAM released *L'école du Micro d'Argent* which sold more than 1 million copies. IAM was known for its "pharaoism"— the rappers used references to Ancient Egypt to champion Arab and African identities at a time when anti-immigrant sentiment was high.

"You need your anger, you transform it and include that in your dance."

Michael Jackson's twists and hat tricks, or jumping into splits like James Brown, whose moves she studied on videotapes. She tried contemporary dance, but remained unimpressed, and only started enjoying herself after taking Afro Jazz dance classes at school.

With hip-hop, however, it was love at first sight. Motin was a teenager when she came across street dance workshops in the 13th arrondissement of Paris, where she lived with her mother at the time.[2] She felt she'd finally found the right fit. "I was very angry as a child, for a long time. I didn't want to get in line, I just wanted to offload, to evacuate that anger, to aaaah!" Motin grimaces with a snarl. "Hip-hop is a dance that allows you to do that. You're there, you get in and, *pah, pah, pah,*" she punches the air, "you need your anger, you transform it and include that in your dance."

Hip-hop wasn't just an outlet for her ire. It was rigorous. It gave her a structure. She needed to practice the steps over and over again for her body to understand the movements. The way they should feel. The way they should flow. She enjoyed the technicality of the body wave, a groove which the French call "smurf." She would break down each trick until she figured out how to perform it, like the windmill—one of the power moves of break dancing—which requires dancers to spin on the floor using their upper body strength alone: "You have to understand how to pull your leg and push on your elbow, otherwise you can't do it, you know?" Motin says. "But there was something very rational about it, something that reassured me. I thought: Okay, I just need to work to get it right."

In the late 1990s, rap music and the culture around it were far from mainstream in France. After school, Motin and a group of friends would train at the local mall, dance in the streets or venture to Châtelet-les Halles, the busiest transport intersection of Paris and the quickest link to the banlieues, then an unofficial meet-up spot for hip-hop battles. The competition was fierce. Yet to this day, Motin's best memories as a dancer remain on the battleground. "I was terrified, and at the same time, when you win a battle, what happens in your body, it's crazy... but when you fail, you pretend it's all good." She lets out a burst of laughter. "That was a bit much, actually. I've distanced myself from that now because I like to be in touch with my emotions—acting tough all the time ended up being a problem for me."

By the time Motin entered university, where she studied literature and psychology, she had joined a professional dance company, Quality Street, as one of its only female members. Being white and a woman was never an issue in the French hip-hop scene, she insists: "In hip-hop, if you're killing it, it doesn't matter if you're black, green, gay or trans.

Motin wears a dress by Marni and trousers by Julia Heuer.

MOVEMENT

"I like to be in touch with my emotions—
acting tough all the time ended up being a problem for me."

If you've done an amazing trick, then you're amazing, that's it. That's what I like about it." Still, in 2009, she created an all-female crew, Swaggers, in order to bring women together, and work off a different kind of energy.

Motin's career as a dancer quickly took off: She was cast in Spanish choreographer Blanca Li's break dance film, *Le Défi*, in the early 2000s, after accompanying her then boyfriend to the auditions. She worked as a backup dancer on television as well as for a number of pop acts, and eventually landed work with choreographers who broadened her horizons, like Sylvain Groud, who, she says, made her realize she could dance to something other than hip-hop. Working with Angelin Preljoçaj, she was inspired by his storytelling, the way he envisioned a full show, not just dance steps.

What many consider the pinnacle of her career—dancing for Madonna—actually had her on the verge of quitting altogether. It was 2012. Motin had gone through the stringent audition process, and landed a coveted place on the Queen of Pop's MDNA tour. She was impressed by the crew's talent and blown away to perform in front of huge crowds day in and day out. Still, she struggled to find meaning in what she was doing. She felt trapped in the moves of hip-hop she'd trained so hard to master. It didn't help that working for one of the world's greatest pop stars meant there was no room for individuality. "I was really happy to be there, but I found myself dancing to choreography that bored me," she says. "And I had to perform it 300 times, without being able to change anything, not even what I did with my little finger, so after a while, yes, it became painful. I realized I didn't want to tell other people's stories anymore."

Coming back from tour, Motin felt she might never dance again. She knew she needed to reconnect with what moved her in order to start moving again. It took her a year. She listened to music that got under her skin, and let herself sway until she found new movements. Gestures that carried meaning because she hadn't learned them; they oozed from her. The verdict was radical: She had to let go of hip-hop music in order to move forward. "I was locked inside of it, I couldn't imagine anything new," she says, circling her eye with her fist. "It was as if I were looking at things this way and then, pfffftttt." Her hand bursts open, widening her field of vision.

This marked the start of Motin's choreographing career. With Swaggers, her crew, she set out to "spill her guts on stage," as she documented it in a 2013 blog post. And so her first show, *In the Middle*, was born. Its opening act set the tone: Motin, dressed in black, enters a dark stage and walks into a lone flash of light, while the intoxicating harmonies of "El Desierto," by the late Mexican American folk singer Lhasa de Sela, fill the room. Suddenly, her body seems possessed, traversed by a magnetic tide pushing her back and forth. Each movement feels impulsive yet controlled, electric yet fluid, as if the waves of hip-hop entered the body of a flamenco dancer. Then, the performance becomes softer. Gradually, more light spots pepper the stage, illuminating other dancers,

whose moves echo Motin's. Their on-and-off synchronicity is hypnotic, until each performer breaks away from the group, each in turn taking the spotlight for a solo, a way to reclaim their individuality. "I do what I want to do, and that's what hip-hop is about too," says Motin. "It's a life philosophy. I may no longer follow hip-hop movements, but I remain profoundly hip-hop. I go wherever my heart beats."

Meeting Belgian musician Stromae did accelerate her heartbeat. So did working with Christine and the Queens. She describes both as visionary artists who conceive their shows as an experience beyond music. They want a say in every detail, be it the lights or the artistic direction, much like Motin does with her own shows. "With them, you know you can drop a choreography, and it will look good, because you think and work together," she says. "Sometimes, when you're not in sync with the artistic director, you look at your choreography and you're like, Crap, this looks like a bad Italian TV show from the 1980s."

Her first time working with Stromae was choreographing the music video of "Papaoutai," a song about growing up without his father, who was killed in the Rwandan genocide. They didn't know each other. Motin filmed him doing improv, then showed him how he moved when he felt awkward. It was much more beautiful than when he tried to do something pretty, she argued. His body needed to reflect his inner state. In the video, Stromae, who is 6'3" and skinny, becomes a motionless mannequin who eventually breaks into an angry dance alongside his younger self. His long body, rattled by convulsions, occasionally shrinks to the ground, becoming the pain-stricken child described in the song. The dance only lasts 20 seconds, but each gesture conveys heartbreak.

Of Christine and the Queens, Motin praises that "she can be gross and fragile and graceful at once." Seeing her dance gives you insight into her soul, she adds: "Dance itself doesn't interest me. What I like about dance is watching people do it. I hate it when a dancer falls like a dancer. I want them to fall like humans do." She approached choreographing *Rouge* the same way. Working with some of the best professionals in the industry, she wanted them to break from the mold, to stop performing like a corps de ballet. "I needed to let them exist as individuals," she says.

Though she is in high demand and constantly traveling, Motin has now settled in Normandy, where she spent the first years of her life, and where she and her partner decided to raise their first child. The show she is preparing in Saint-Lô, a city of fewer than 20,000 residents, allows her once again to create something that is fully hers, working with eight dancers and an actor on stage. Sometimes, she says, she still feels nothing, when she's dancing. Occasionally, she gets frustrated. And then, there are times when each part of her body feels alive, each movement gives her pleasure. She closes her eyes and rolls her head. "It's wonderful. You're in the moment and … you're just a body, you feel what's inside, it's like you can become anything you want," she whispers. "Whoa."

Previous Spread: Motin wears a top, trousers, sweater and dress by Baserange. Left: Motin wears a dress Victoria Beckham.

Birdwatching:
Jason Ward

Whether trapped in a bad situation or just terrible traffic, watching birds in flight has always helped naturalist *Jason Ward* unwind. *Amanda Avutu* joins him for a walk through an Atlanta park. Photography by *Corey Woosley*

As a child growing up in the Bronx, Jason Ward was an astute observer. He'd watch people moving through the streets with curiosity, wanting to know their stories, but also did so out of necessity. "My father always taught me to be hyperaware of your surroundings. Always know what's going on a block ahead of you and a block behind you," he tells me. We are standing at the edge of Lake Clara Meer in Atlanta's Piedmont Park, where Ward, the 33-year-old host of the YouTube series *Birds of North America*,[1] and former apprentice at the National Audubon Society, was first formally introduced to birding. In 2013, Ward, who worked at a mortgage company, got a promotion that left him with a little extra free time and money. The lifelong animal enthusiast Googled organizations in Atlanta and stumbled upon Atlanta Audubon. With a cheap pair of binoculars, he met a group of people for a birding walk and fell in love. Ward crowdsourced his birding knowledge, devouring books, videos and apps. Within eight months, he was leading the walks, and still does—the first Saturday of every month.

Joggers rush by us, French tourists gather to take a photo, a woman asks her toddler if he wants a snack. "There's a robin singing," Ward says, and suddenly I can, in fact, hear a robin singing. "There's a flicker calling out. It was that single high note. That piercing sound," Ward says, pausing. The tourists laugh and snap another photo. The woman tells the toddler, "Dog! Look at the doggie!" It is nature and city. It is chaos and calm. Ward sets up his scope, draws up his binoculars, opens his ears and centers himself.

"There!" He's pointing across the lake. "That's a flicker. Woodpeckers have this bouncy flight. There's flashes of yellow underneath, see?" Listening to Ward is like tuning into a different frequency, one that turns the volume down on the static fuzz of life. "Grackle," he says confidently, "The grackle sounds like a rusty gate." Now that I know what to listen for and what to block out, it does.

Ward first realized that birds could transport him when he was 15. One day, while living in a Bronx homeless shelter with his family, the teen noticed feathers floating by the window. Ward moved closer and the drama came into focus: a peregrine falcon eating a pigeon. In that moment, everything except for the predator and prey receded and he was transported out of the homeless shelter, out of the city, out of reality. Fifteen-odd years later, the peregrine falcon remains a constant force in Ward's life. He lifts his binoculars to his face, looks up at the edge of the park—jagged with tall buildings—where the bird of prey might make its perch here in Atlanta. "This bird is a survivor. Fifty-plus years ago it was on the verge of extinction. And now it's doing really well, *thriving* in environments that it's not supposed to thrive in," Ward explains.[2] He describes how the falcon dives at breakneck speeds, extending its talons mid-flight to punch the pigeon as it passes by. "They can leave an undesirable situation in search of greener pastures at the flick of a wing," he says. "I wanted to be able to do that."

"The New Yorker in me always wants to go... And I have to remind myself to slow down for a second."

NOTES

1. Each episode of *Birds of North America* runs to just under 10 minutes and sees Ward spend time with other members of the US birding community, such as the Feminist Bird Club. His younger brother Jeffrey, who shares his hobby, also makes guest appearances.
—
—

2. In the 1960s, not a single peregrine falcon was found east of the Mississippi River. In 1970, however, The Peregrine Fund at Cornell University began a program to bring the birds back to the East Coast. Now, at least 17 breeding pairs live within the borders of New York City's five boroughs—the densest known population of urban peregrines in the world.

Ward says that the beauty of birding lies in its ability to affect our experience of space and time. "You're moving at a much slower pace. Taking in the sights and sounds around you," he explains. And yet, he struggles against this slowing. "The New Yorker in me always wants to *go*. Even when I'm birding, I always want to see the next bird. I find myself walking at a pace that's my typical walking pace while I have binoculars around my neck. And I have to remind myself to slow down for a second."

"When things are relaxed and calm and I'm in a great mood, I'll come out here and I'll set a goal for myself. Let's see 50 species today. Which is very doable. Let's just be at one with your environment. Let's just be present," he says. But when Ward is in a darker place, he doesn't observe the birds' world so much as he immerses himself in it. "In those situations, I'll find myself spending more time. Just allowing myself to be in the moment and observe what they're doing. It distracts me. And it calms me down."

Ward points out that there's a tension between finding relaxation in the movement of birds, and understanding that those movements are often motivated by the animal's stress. "None of a bird's movements are stress free. They're always aware. Is there a hawk around me? Is there something that could end my life?" he says.

An ambulance siren's wail crescendos, eclipsing the sound of the Canada geese flapping, the mallards diving, the grackles making their rusted gate sound. As the siren recedes, Ward lifts his binoculars to his face. "There's a red-tailed hawk. It's young. It doesn't have a red tail yet. Its tail is brown and banded. Now that particular bird was probably born last year." He watches it circle behind the skeletal branches of a tree, and translates for me: "When he's circling, he's rising on thermals. There's an invisible pocket of warm air that's rising and he's utilizing that to gain altitude." When he drops the binoculars, you can see in his eyes a profound respect for what the bird has endured to survive its first year.

"Let's go to my favorite place here, the Wetlands," Ward says. As we walk, he tells me that when he was growing up, he was inspired by nature show hosts like the Kratt Brothers and the Crocodile Hunter, but longed for a naturalist who looked like him. "Kids gravitate toward images they can relate to: 'He looks like me, I can do that.' But if I turn on Nat Geo and there's no one that looks like me, I wonder, Is this something that's available to me? Can I do this? I want to change that."

We walk amid joggers and nearly collide with a careening biker, before passing a babbling creek and entering the calm of the Wetlands. "This is the part of the park I could just sit in," Ward says. He tells me he could close his eyes, and know we are near wetlands because the rusty blackbirds, winter wrens, waterthrushes, owls, and red-shouldered hawks tell him so. "You have to be able to identify birds by their sound before you even see them," he explains. "Singing is a way to say one of two things, either 'This is my territory, don't enter,' or 'I'm looking for a mate.'"

We stand for a while, just listening, before walking back out of the Wetlands. When we reach the sidewalk, a precipice between the natural and urban worlds, Ward points to the top of a tall tree. "There's a hawk's nest up there," he says. Throngs of people move beneath the nest, unaware of the giant bird circling above them, surviving. "If I could, I'd set up a scope and watch that nest and try to get everyone that passed by to take a look."

So much of what Ward wants is simple: for people to stop, breathe, see, listen and notice the natural world around them. "I was sitting one day in bad bumper-to-bumper traffic," he begins, "when I noticed about five or six barn swallows. These beautiful, acrobatic birds are just swooping around between cars, over the cars, catching insects. Immediately I'm like, It's not so bad. I'm sitting in traffic and I'm not moving anywhere, but these birds are putting on a show and I'm enjoying it. Then I wonder, 'How many other people are seeing this? How many other people are enjoying this as well?' In my head, I step out of the car, step up to a podium with a mic and tell their story." Ward might not have been able to reach his fellow commuters that day, but he stands at the proverbial podium every day on his YouTube channel, through his guided walks at Piedmont Park, and his lectures across the country. And the stories he can tell you? Well, they'll transport you right out of whatever frustrates you, right out of your seat, right out of reality.

RODERICK

In Berlin, Stephanie d'Arc Taylor meets the man who makes music move—orchestra conductor Roderick Cox. Photography by Dennis Weber

The stereotypical orchestra conductor is a broody spirit—a whirlwind of wild hair, flashing eyes and melodramatic physicality. But the award-winning conductor Roderick Cox has struck a chord, despite his perfectly sensible haircut. At age 32, he has already performed (or will debut this year) with orchestras in Los Angeles, Paris, London and New York.

Over cappuccinos near his home in Berlin, Cox took exception to the idea that conducting is defined by physical histrionics. Rather, the success of a conductor is determined by whether they can develop an opinion on a piece of music, and convince an orchestra to tell a new version of an old story. As a black man from Georgia, Cox's profile offers the overwhelmingly white world of classical music a new perspective: A 2014 study by the League of American Orchestras found that less than 2% of musicians and just over 4% of conductors in American orchestras are black. Plenty of people are passionate about classical music, and plenty of musicians perform at an international level. It's the ability to interpret the language of music, Cox says, using one's own experiences as a conduit, that makes for world-class conductors. After all, literally speaking, a conductor is something through which energy is transferred. Judging from his performances, there's a fair amount of eye-flashing too.

SDT: *You're from Macon, Georgia, which is not the first place that comes to mind when we think of classical music.* **RC:** There have been some amazing artists to come out of Macon, Georgia! The music is rich there, from Otis Redding, the Allman Brothers, Little Richard, and so forth.

SDT: *Was music a big part of your life growing up?* **RC:** We were huge churchgoers, so I was with music all the time. Not classical, but gospel. That's how my mom would wake us up in the morning. I also benefited from a really robust music education program in my elementary school. I remember that first day vividly: We went into a classroom and tried out real instruments. The band director assigned me percussion but I changed to French horn in high school.

SDT: *When you were a kid, what did you think a conductor's job was?* **RC:** Our band director was an educator, so I thought I wanted to be an educator. Now I'm the organizer—you've got the calendars, the trips, you're seeing who's here, etc.

SDT: *Forgive this question, but what does a conductor actually do?* **RC:** It seems we have to answer this question a lot. Conductors need to have a huge amount of knowledge of not only the music, but the instruments. Usually we've played many of them, if not mastered them. You're working with experts in all their fields. How do you put all those experts together?

SDT: *And what's the conductor an expert in?* **RC:** We're experts on the orchestra as a collective. We have all the instrument parts in our heads. A first violinist playing in an orchestra only sees their part; they might not know what the tuba is doing. We're able to coordinate what everyone is doing to make the story cohesive. Most importantly, you have to have something meaningful to say about the music. You're not just showing that the orchestra can play a piece of music. That's what makes the performance exceptional.

"*I've pulled muscles. I have to stretch before and after concerts.*"

SDT: *You can have performances that are technically perfect, but—* **RC:** Boring!

SDT: *Technically perfect, but not opinionated.* **RC:** Yes, exactly. As a kid from Macon, Georgia, sometimes I think, Who are you to have an opinion on this Brahms symphony? You try to use the information you have, and your knowledge of the composer and their culture to strengthen that interpretation.

SDT: *It's a very physical job. Have you ever been injured on the podium?* **RC:** I've pulled muscles. I have to stretch before and after concerts. I see a massage therapist and a chiropractor.

SDT: *At the gym do you work on certain muscle groups?* **RC:** I have to be careful at the gym. Many guys are about bulking up their chest, but I need range of motion with my arms. When you're trying to get a soft, beautiful sound out of an orchestra, it's a little weird if you look like The Rock.

SDT: *Could you do your job sitting down?* **RC:** Certain conductors do conduct sitting down. As long as the hands are visible to the orchestra and there's eye contact.

SDT: *What about with your eyes closed?* **RC:** I haven't seen too many conductors conduct with their eyes closed, except Herbert von Karajan [the Austrian conductor who led the Berlin Philharmonic for over three decades]. I feel like that would throw me off balance! I would fall over.

SDT: *Why don't rock bands need conductors?* **RC:** They have a rhythm section that keeps a beat. You have that in jazz bands, you have that in pop music—it's the simple rhythm underneath it all. In most classical music, that's not the case. It's an unstable rhythm.

SDT: *Most conductors seem to have very striking faces—Esa-Pekka Salonen's aquiline nose, or Zubin Mehta's hypnotizing eyes. Does it help to have an expressive face?* **RC:** It's not so much about being expressive. There's something quite mag-

ical, I can't put my finger on it.... There's a telepathic thing that's happening—you have to find a way to show people your soul. That's tough to teach. It's the difference between looking at someone while they're talking, and really listening to them. Orchestras can tell. That's the line between good conductors and okay conductors. We're not the smartest or the most knowledgeable, but we're able to communicate to the orchestras what's in our brains, what's in our hearts and souls through our gestures.

SDT: *What would happen if a conductor walked off the stage mid-performance?* **RC:** Um, for what reason? **SDT:** *If they were about to be sick, maybe?* **RC:** Well, the orchestra would have to stop! But there's a cover conductor who's ready to get on stage at a moment's notice. It's an expensive thing if the show can't go on. There have been cases, depending on the repertoire, where orchestras have managed

to have the concertmaster [the first violin, to the left of the conductor] lead from the front stand.

SDT: *Is the vocabulary of conducting standardized, or do you put your own spin on it?* **RC:** Much of it is standardized. But when you're working with a new orchestra, they have to get to know your specific vocabulary. The first rehearsal is when I learn about the orchestra and they learn about me. That's why first rehearsals are usually closed to audiences.

SDT: *It's a symbiotic relationship between the orchestra and a conductor, learning about each other and growing together. Where does the audience fit into that?* **RC:** One thing I've learned is that an audience member anywhere in the world can see when something special is happening on stage. As classical musicians, we should try our best to give our audience members that magnetism, because that's what keeps us relevant. When we do it well, audiences get it.

"You have to find a way to show people your soul. That's tough to teach."

Essay:

Run for Your Life

Words by Debika Ray

The amateur athlete has had an image overhaul. The same weekend joggers who once lapped the local park are setting their sights on grueling tests of endurance: desert overnighters, mountain traverses and weeklong rainforest runs. Debika Ray meets the white-collar workers giving up their vacations to participate in races that prioritize mental stamina—and money—over physical fitness.

"It's one of the sports that can destroy your ego more devastatingly than anything else—on top of a mountain, in the dark, after 25 hours of running." Adharanand Finn is talking to me about the subject of his 2019 book, *The Rise of the Ultra Runners*, which charts the growing popularity and appeal of extreme races that take place over hundreds of kilometers in some of the harshest conditions on earth. He recalls the first time he participated in one—a six-day, 165-kilometer run across the Oman desert. "Initially I was doing quite well, but then I completely fell apart—mentally and physically—and I was nearly last toward the end," he says.

Finn came to ultrarunning on a journalistic assignment, after having competed in several marathons and shorter endurance races. Since then he has done several more and, while he doesn't consider himself a true convert, he has started to understand the appeal. As he puts it: "The experience you get by spending 15 hours at a time running, often in extreme environments, can lead to quite intense feeling of highs and lows."

Trekking miles across hostile environments—whether on foot, horseback or water—is as old as humanity itself, but the popularity of such races as a leisure pursuit has grown rapidly in recent years. Listing websites such as Run Ultra have reported a 1,000% jump in the number of these events—from a 24-day, 850-kilometer slog across the Nepalese Himalayas to a 6-day, 236-kilometer jaunt across the Costa Rican rainforest—over the past decade or so. In February, running shoe review website RunRepeat and the International Association of Ultrarunners published the *State of Ultra Running 2020* report, which they claim is the largest of its kind. It revealed that participation in ultramarathons has risen by 1,676% over the past 23 years and 345% in just 10 years—to 611,098 runs each year. Similarly punishing events that include sports other than running, such as the Ironman Triathlon and Tough Mudder obstacle race, are also booming.[1]

It's a phenomenon that has partly been fueled by social media, where those who succeed in finishing inspire others to reach the starting line. "When I've asked people how they came to ultrarunning, many say they saw it on Facebook," Finn says. But the dopamine rush from online likes is not enough to keep you going through a race. Interestingly, its popularity isn't attributed to the wider growth of wellness culture—not least because excessive exercise isn't particularly good for your body. In fact, fitness does not seem to be particularly relevant to ultrarunners: In a 2018 study, 1,394 people were asked if they'd quit the sport if they knew for sure that it was bad for their health and 74% said "no."[2] This chimes with Finn's experience. "The motivating factor for an ultramarathon is not health," he says.

1. The first Ironman was held in Hawaii in 1978, with 15 competitors. Today, there are close to 200 races from which to choose. Because an Ironman Triathlon involves swimming and biking as well as running, the cost of buying the necessary equipment can range from $5,000 to $24,000. There are even special triathlon bikes designed to angle the body to reduce drag.

—

—

2. Short-term health complications associated with ultramarathons include vomiting, blurry vision (due to wind damage) and sleep deprivation. In the long-term, ultramarathon runners are more likely to experience heart problems.

So what is? Perhaps some light can be shed by considering the type of people who seem to be attracted to ultra-endurance events. *The State of Ultra Running* has some numbers: 77% of participants are men, compared with 62% in standard marathons; the average age is 42, compared with 40 in marathons. Most runners come from France (12.4%), the US (12.1%) and South Africa (6.7%). In Finn's experience, they tend to be white—an interesting observation given the dominance of East African countries in more conventional long-distance events.

There's another trend: the popularity of endurance events among affluent white-collar workers. Races such as the 254-kilometer UVU Jungle Marathon in the Amazon, the 4 Deserts Series of runs across deserts around the world and the Grand to Grand Ultra 268-kilometer race from the Grand Canyon to Las Vegas, for example, are believed to draw 20% to 30% of participants from the financial sector. Meanwhile, organizations such as Ironman run specific challenges for business executives. "Somebody described these to me as a holiday for CEOs," Finn says.

Some of this is quite simply down to money—the notorious Marathon des Sables, for example, costs more than $5,000 for the privilege of lugging your own food and belongings 251 kilometers across the Moroccan Sahara for six days. The appeal may reflect a yearning to disconnect in our highly networked world. "I don't take a phone with me, so there are roughly nine days where I have no contact with the outside world," says 48-year-old Martin Mack, president of construction business Concord Homes in Canada, who is gearing up for his sixth Marathon des Sables.

For these runners, modern life is a state of continuous comfort, as they yo-yo between warm, clean shelter and safe, efficient transportation. In the Sahara, Mack says, there's none of that. "There are just three types of terrain: sand, rock, and sand and rock mixed. There's little vegetation and no escape from the

"We have a sense of being removed from the world. Sometimes you need a bit of physical suffering to feel like you're fulfilling your body's expectations."

sun—when you're out there for six or eight hours a day, there's no shade to hide under." Unlike in the business world, there is no prospect of control: "You're at the mercy of the weather, the terrain and your body. It doesn't matter how good a shape you're in—sometimes you can mentally fall apart. The most appealing part is pushing yourself to your breaking point, then going beyond that."

Finn believes this yearning for a rawer form of human experience is why people who have attained material success gravitate toward such events. "As humans, we're born with an expectation of dealing with our environment, and when we don't have to, we have a sense of being removed from the world and missing out on something. Sometimes you need a bit of physical suffering to feel like you're fulfilling your body's expectations," Finn says. The punishing impact of these races seems to be central. "People talk about descending into 'the pain cave' and struggling to get through that—they really relish that moment of suffering," he continues.

To reinforce the point, Finn recalls running an ultramarathon with a Kenyan professional athlete, who called it a day when he hurt his toe. "He wasn't there to suffer—he was there to feel good and strong and the moment that stopped, he stopped." It's an incident he feels illustrates a difference in motivation between people for whom running is mainly a professional sport and those who have taken it up as an extreme test of body and mind.

There are parallels between the logistical challenges posed by extreme endurance events and the control-and-conquer mentality of the corporate world. "It's essentially management and problem-solving—you manage your food, your water intake, your salt intake, your pace," Mack says. Ultrarunning and capitalism also share a belief in continual human progress—that greater success is attainable and that we can always have more, if only we crack the formula. The question is, how much further can we push ourselves?

A dance party for one spirals into another dimension. Photography by Pelle Crépin @ Styling by Katy Lassen

SECOND TIME AROUND

Above: Aurelie wears a top and trousers by Pleats Please Issey Miyake and shoes by Bottega Veneta.
Right: She wears a top by Jil Sander, trousers by Hermès and a hat by Jacquemus at Matches Fashion. Previous: She wears a top and skirt by Roksanda.

Right: Aurelie wears a dress by Christopher Kane. Above: She wears a dress by Mulberry.

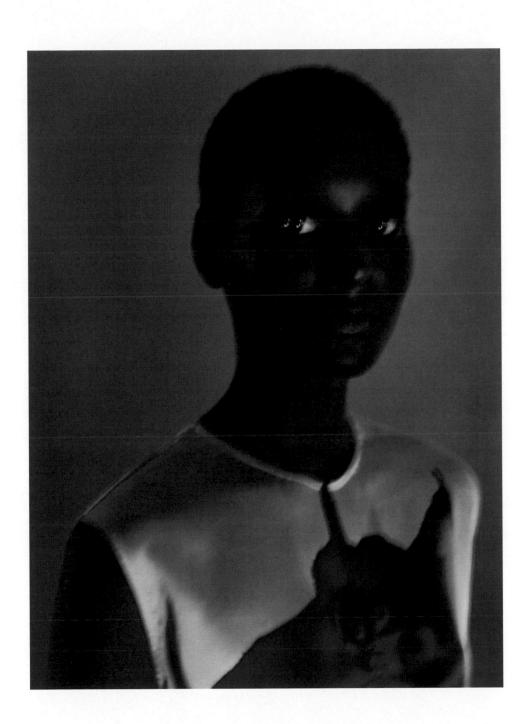

Left: Aurelie wears a jacket and trousers from Preen by Thornton Bregazzi and earrings by Christopher Kane. Above: She wears a dress by Colville.

Not many architects skate for their country, and not many skateboarders design the parks they skate in. Kyla Marshell meets the woman at the center of an unusual Venn diagram.

ALEXIS

Photography by Dominik Tarabanski

"I see skating as an imaginative misuse of space."

When Alexis Sablone finds a moment to chat, she's not coming from the skate park but from her art studio, where she's got a sculpture made from tree branches underway. The seven-time X Games medalist, who started skating competitively when she was just 12, also has an undergraduate and master's degree in architecture and practices out of New York. It's a career hybrid that's led to some imaginative results, including her design of a skate park, more aptly described as a "skateable sculpture" in Malmö, Sweden. She called the experience a "dream project"—but in everyday life, she finds ways of staying creative, whether through her art, which also includes animation, or the invention of new tricks on her board. All being well, she'll soon encounter the biggest adventure in her 20-year career: representing the US in skateboarding's debut at the Olympic Games in Tokyo. (When we speak, the tournament's postponement to 2021 has not yet been announced.)

KM: *How are you feeling about the Olympics? It'll be your first time and the first time for skateboarding* **AS:** A mix of nervous and excited. I have no idea what to expect. I still have some qualifiers ahead of me. I can't think about the actual thing yet.

KM: *You've said you view skating as an art form because of the inventiveness it takes to find places to skate. Do you think of yourself as an artist who's doing something physical, or an athlete with creative leanings?* **AS:** When I started skateboarding in the '90s, no skateboarders referred to themselves as athletes. [Being an athlete] was kind of like an insult because we felt we were different. At this point, with the Olympics, there are so many different sides to skateboarding. [The Olympics] is the competition side. When I'm doing that, it feels very much like a sport, like I'm an athlete looking at a scoreboard. But when I'm skating street and trying to film something, that feels really different.

KM: *What's the connective tissue for you between architecture and skateboarding?* **AS:** I feel a lot of overlap between architecture and skating in creative uses of space. With architecture, you're trying to imagine space that isn't there. In skateboarding, you're taking what's around you and trying to reimagine different ways to use that space.

Skateboarders have a certain eye. You're constantly looking at the materiality and shape and how everything around you is organized because you're looking at it to try to choreograph something through it.

KM: *Are you at all inspired by dancers?* **AS:** At Barnard [where Sablone completed her undergraduate degree], I had a lot of friends that were dancers. I was describing skateboarding as choreography through space, and I think that's exactly what it is. There's a certain rhythm and pace when you have an idea for a trick, and you're imagining it, and I think that's choreography.

KM: *One perception of skateboarders is that they're a public nuisance. But as you said, part of the art of skating is seeing spaces in a unique way. How do you think about repurposed versus dedicated space for skaters?* **AS:** I think they're both important. When I started skateboarding, there wasn't a skate park in my town. I had to drive about an hour to get to one. Even in the years I've lived in New York, there are so many more skate parks everywhere. They're fun, and I think they're a great place for people to

As a young woman, Sablone resisted the pull of LA that draws so many skaters. New York felt like a better fit for someone with her mixed portfolio.

MOVEMENT

"Skateboarders have a certain eye. You're constantly looking at how everything is organized because you're looking to choreograph something through it."

meet up. But that doesn't mean that they replace spots that are part of the city. Because found or reclaimed space—there's something about that. I see it as a playful and imaginative misuse of space rather than vandalism or anything negative. Always having something to search for is really important, and a fundamental part of skateboarding. If something's built for you, it's fun to practice on but it's not the same thing. The spots where you choose to skate say a lot about you.

KM: *Did you ever feel like architecture was the "respectable" or safe thing to do?* **AS:** Not for me. I loved school. I wanted to study, and be in that environment. [But] when

I got out of school the last thing I wanted was a conventional job, and skateboarding gave me a way to make money and buy time so I could work on my own projects, have my own schedule and travel around the world. Now that skateboarding's going to be in the Olympics, it's never felt so credible.

KM: *Do you still encounter people who don't take it seriously?* **AS:** It's a really pleasant surprise to people because they're not expecting to hear [that I'm a skateboarder]. They just think it's cool and wonder what that entails. But also as I've gotten older there is sometimes the response of, "Oh, you're still doing that?" which is what it is. I always think that has

something to do with being a female.

KM: *You designed a skate park in Malmö, Sweden. What was that experience like?* **AS:** There's a really vibrant skate scene there. [A friend I met there] works in the city council of Malmö and is also a skateboarder, so he asked me if I was interested in designing a skateable sculpture. In some ways, it was a dream project for me because it was not a skate park but basically a large-scale public art sculpture that's open to different user groups. It's open to skateboarders, and other people in the city can interact with it. It can be shared by different people. I think there should be more spaces like that.

KM: *Do you have any insight into*

how architecture, skating or art can be activated for social movements, or change? **AS:** It used to be rare that you saw another girl skater. I didn't skate with other girls until I was an adult. You go to a skate park now and it's still 99% guys. For some people, that can be intimidating. [But] in the last few years that's changed dramatically, and there are a lot more women skateboarding now. I skate for Converse and have been involved in both of their Pride campaigns since I started. On a smaller scale, I try to be encouraging. Being a queer female professional skateboarder, I try to use my voice however I can to make sure everybody knows that skateboarding is for everybody.

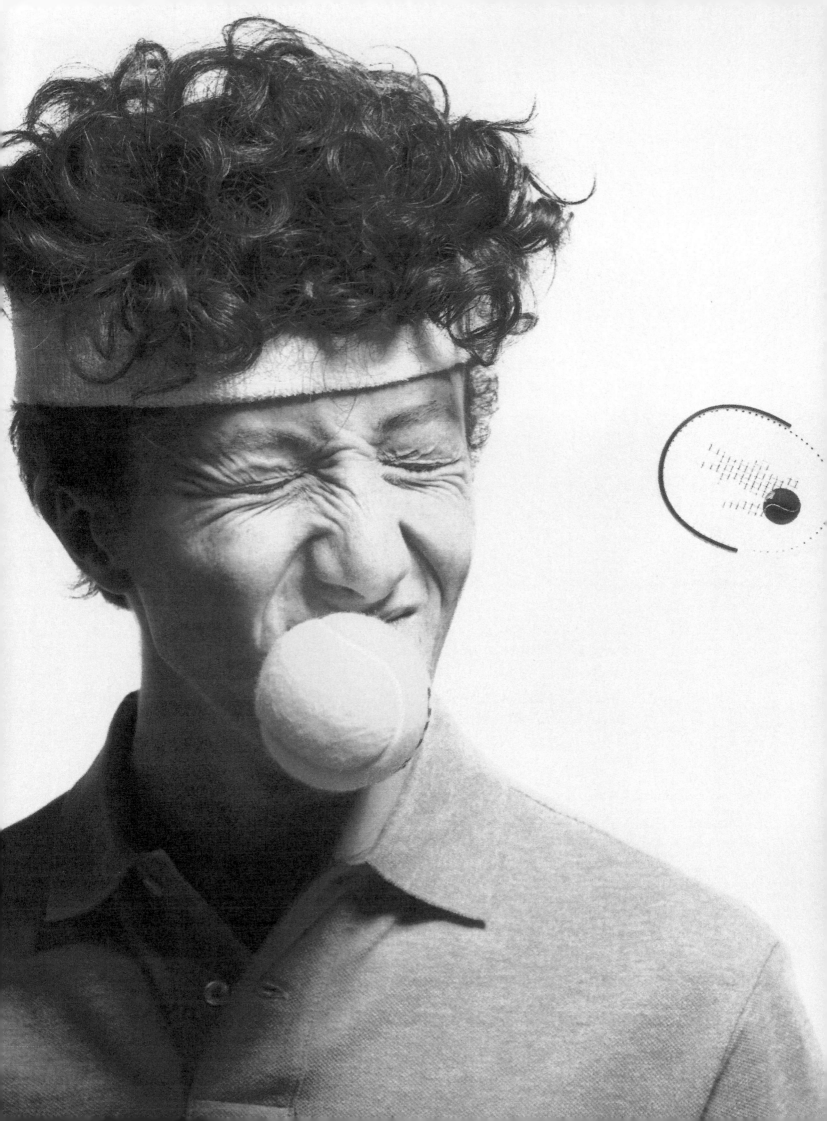

GAME

Keep your eye on the prize—and the ball. Photography by Luc Braquet and Styling by Camille-Joséphine Teisseire.

FACE

Left to Right: Simon wears a polo shirt and trousers by Lacoste and a cap by Ellesse. Racket by Lacoste and ball by Rado; Lamin wears shorts by Hermès, socks by Falke and sneakers by NikeCourt Vapor x TC Knit; Lamin wears a polo shirt by Le Coq Sportif, shorts by EA7, socks and sneakers by Polo Ralph Lauren, a cap by Ellesse and a watch by Casio. Balls by Lacoste. Previous: Jimmy wears a polo shirt by Polo Ralph Lauren and a headband by Ellesse. Lamin wears a shirt by Uniqlo, shorts by La Sportiva and wristbands by Ellesse.

Left to Right: Simon wears a sweatshirt by Polo Ralph Lauren, and shorts and a headband by Ellesse;
Simon wears a polo shirt by Lacoste, and shorts, cap and a watch by Hermès; Lamin wears shorts by EA7 and socks and sneakers by
Polo Ralph Lauren. All tennis rackets and balls by Lacoste.

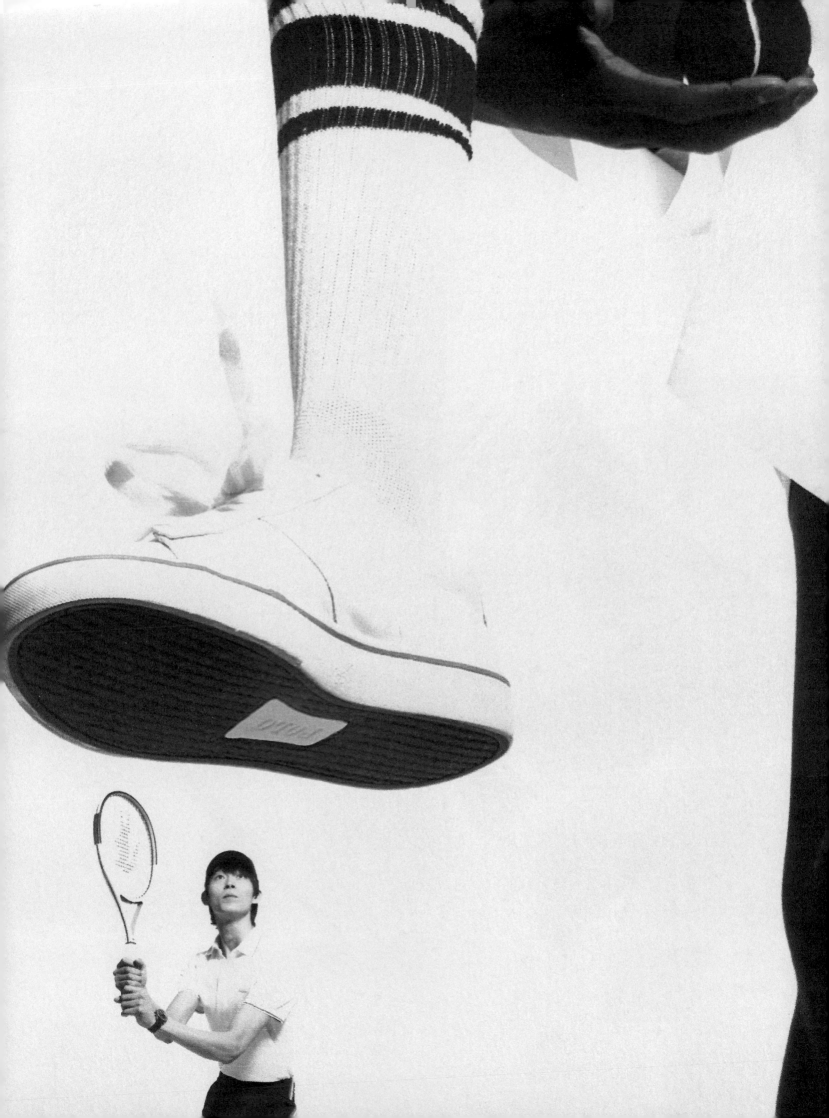

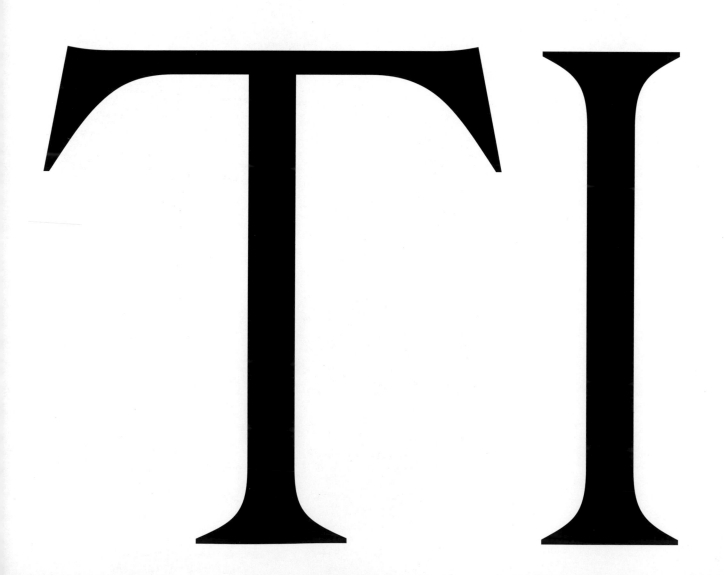

Stop Moving

Sometimes it seems like all is movement: a maelstrom of obligations, work and opportunity. The constant, powerful flow of life can feel invigorating but exhausting too. Work follows us home, and free time fills with domestic responsibilities, social commitments, fitness goals and keeping up with the rush of information. Rest becomes an indulgent waste of precious time.

Seventy years ago, the philosopher Josef Pieper argued that we have developed a "prejudice that comes from overvaluing the sphere of work." This prejudice has clouded our sense for the value of leisure, which for other cultures and other times, he says, "is the center point about which everything revolves." Our prejudice has only increased as it has become easier to work whenever and wherever we want. Late 20th-century technologies have made us more efficient but haven't freed up time for leisure because we have used them—both the time and the technology—to do more work. In the face of this, philosopher of technology Albert Borgmann observes, "happiness appears to decline as technological affluence rises." Borgmann's view complements Pieper's assertion that "despair and the incapac-ity for leisure are twins." Life beleaguered by constant occupation is exhausting and calls for a pause to read or think. It needs rest.

Even so, one of our favorite forms of leisure—sport—seems to offer just the opposite. Intensive exercise complements work with more activity. But in sports, too, athletes and physiologists have begun to discover the crucial value of rest. When athletes overtrain, their physical and mental fitness decrease. Fatigue sets in; ambition declines; moods worsen. The principal remedy is rest. It may seem odd to take advice about rest from someone who once ran 350 miles at a stretch over three sleepless nights, but ultra-endurance runner Dean Karnazes attests first-hand that "too much exercise can put your body in a constant state of restlessness or on high alert."

He points out that rest not only calms this agitation, but it also improves performance, prevents injury, promotes muscle recovery, fortifies the immune system and "helps to recharge the psyche." He advises weekly days off, but this kind of restfulness doesn't come naturally. It takes a new mindset to prioritize time off, to step out of the ceaseless flow of commitments, ambitions and information.

Stay Balanced

"Sit straight." "Don't slouch." "Relax your shoulders." "Chin up." We receive such a barrage of posture-related instructions in our childhood that it's easy to believe the wisdom is absolute. Correct posture is associated with upright morality and upstanding character. Slumping, leaning, fidgeting is the preserve of the feckless, while overly tense shoulders and back signal an inability to tolerate stress.

If that were true, then controlling your physical deportment would equate to self-control. That's perhaps why the Alexander Technique has remained popular for more than 100 years. It's a therapy that aims to change the way you hold and use your body in order to tackle long-standing physical and mental problems, including pain and stress, as well as making you more calm and confident. "Whether you need help with posture, balance or movement, input into skills and interests—or if you simply wish to gain more control over your life—the Alexander Technique offers a great way for you to make the changes you seek," informs the Professional Association of Alexander Teachers, which helps people learn how not to "pull yourself out of shape."

It started out as a method of self-improvement for actors. Australian thespian Frederick Matthias Alexander was experiencing problems with his voice, so he spent years looking in the mirror, observing his body's movements and their effect on his vocal performance, and adapting to improve them. He eventually ended up teaching his technique in London to the likes of George Bernard Shaw and Aldous Huxley. Today, like with most alternative therapies, medical institutions are noncommittal about its efficacy: Britain's National Health Service says it's "safe and poses no health risks," but points out that many of its supposed benefits are unproven.

It's interesting that the Alexander Technique is far less absolutist about posture than one might assume. Tackling bad habits is part of it, but teachers also emphasize adaptation and flexibility—there is no one correct approach that fits all. In that respect, the Alexander Technique seems more in keeping with current trends in how we think about the body and the self—we're not so much malleable objects living up to external standards but independent beings with unique needs, tendencies and capabilities. The technique's focus on self-awareness, personal autonomy and on being mindful of triggers, as well as its practical, problem-solving ethos, have a distinctly contemporary feel. The question still remains: When mind is pitted against matter, can the latter really win?

What can the Alexander Technique teach us?
Words by *Debika Ray*

It can be tempting to think of human beings as living lives of either mind or body. Or it can feel like the interior life is the true and real life, while the body is just a container for the brain. This is an especially understandable reaction to being physically awkward—sloppy, imprecise—when your mind is comparatively agile.

No wonder so many of us find dancing a daunting prospect. The idea of moving not just for prosaic reasons like transport, or for the satisfaction of athletic achievement, but purely for joy, for artistry, for abandon—what could be more repulsive for the inwardly inclined? There's a reason that, so often, people only dance when drunk, at times of high drama and high intoxication like a wedding. In his film *Happy End*, Michael Haneke explores the relationship between alcohol and dance in a darkly compelling scene—Pierre Laurent, the son of a wealthy patriarch with addiction issues, performs Sia's "Chandelier" at karaoke and accompanies it with a grimly transfixing, jarringly impassioned dance. The abandon, unearned by sober intention, is not joyous but troubling. But dance can also open doors into strange new worlds. In the Greek film *Dogtooth*, sisters who are kept in perpetual childhood by their father perform a typically staid dance for him, but one signals her desire to break out of his prison by trying out modern, sexualized moves she has seen covertly on VHS tapes. *Call Me By Your Name* shows us Oliver and Elio at the village disco, losing themselves in an ecstasy of goofy exuberance that mirrors their growing mutual lust. In *Saturday Night Fever*, John Travolta's Tony transcends the limitations of his class and family background through his disco moves.

One way to dance more is to reframe it, to consider it a practice not divergent from, but continuous with, the act of thinking. To move your body in dance is not an act divorced from cognition—you are not abandoning your body, leaving it alone without its mind. Instead, think of dancing as its own distinct kind of thought. When we walk through a new place, moving our body with intention and curiosity, we come to know it in a different way than if we were to only see it on a map. When we dance, then, we are knowing the world in a different way: Thinking with our whole selves.

Dance More

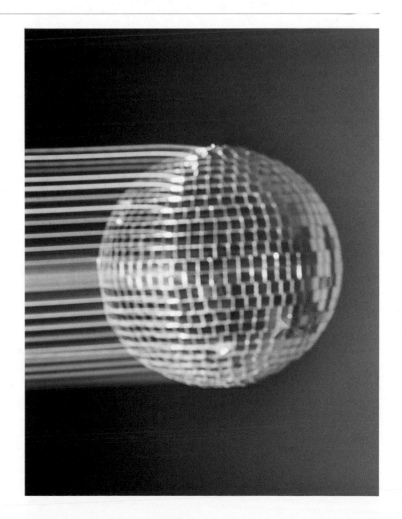

How to move without mortification.
Words by *Megan Nolan*

Write Movement

How do you capture something as ephemeral as dance on paper? This is the question posed by choreologists, who notate dance. Alison Curtis-Jones is a choreologist at the Trinity Laban Conservatoire of Music and Dance in London. She specializes in the work of Rudolf Laban, a modern dance pioneer, and researches the idea of the human body as a dynamic archive of movement.

TF: *How do you put dance on a page?* **ACJ:** You can record music using marks on paper, but during Laban's time there was nothing similar for movement. He looked at how our bodies are organized and devised a system to record movement, later called Labanotation, in 1918.

TF: *What does it look like?* **ACJ:** It's a series of bars across paper. The body is the vertical axis, and symbols represent direction, level and duration of movement. These go further out for extremities: On the inside are bars representing your core, legs and head. As you move out, there are your arms, from shoulder to elbows, wrists, hands and fingers.

TF: *Are there other dance languages?* **ACJ:** Another is Benesh notation, created by Rudolf Benesh and primarily used to record ballet. It goes across the page like a music score, from left to right.

TF: *Did Laban's notation stick?* **ACJ:** Laban actually moved away from his system because it didn't adequately reflect dynamics. You can get a sense of timing and duration but not effort: whether a movement is strong or light. He later came up with a different system that accounted for force.

TF: *Is notation still relevant today?* **ACJ:** It takes a lot of time and a trained eye to notate a whole movement phrase, so today it's used less and less. We don't teach it anymore at my conservatoire. There's also the question of technology: Why bother with notation when we can record a video on our phones?

TF: *What do you do in your daily work?* **ACJ:** I look at the lost choreographic work of Laban, dance works for which we have no tangible records. I'm looking at critical reviews and photographs and reimagining his works for the present day.

TF: *What is the value of unearthing dance history?* **ACJ:** The history of dance is short compared to other art forms. It's incredible we don't take more concern with it. You wouldn't train to be an actor and not learn about Shakespeare.

TF: *How was dance passed on before notation?* **ACJ:** With ballet classics like *Swan Lake*, they were handed from person to person. Dancers' bodies are archives. They carry history—archiving experiences, training, dynamics, expressivity and understanding of space. Yet now I'm wondering: Is bodily memory being outsourced to phones? So when I restage my work, I rarely let my dancers look at film footage. It comes from their bodily memory.

TF: *The idea of a lost dance is quite poignant—do you believe that, for all its disadvantages, video technology at least means we won't lose any more dances?* **ACJ:** I think we're at the point of saturation. People can record everything now. That brings an impermanence—we move on to new things so quickly. In the past there were seminal works and you had to go to the theater because there was no other way to see them. Now all work, professional or amateur, is posted on YouTube.

Step in Time

Rewind to the celebrity workout video craze.
Words by *Stephanie d'Arc Taylor*

"I never loved aerobics," says Cher, right before she launches into a step class involving swoops, kicks, jumps and a heart-rate check-in. The year is 1991. Cher is resplendent in sheer black tights, a black leotard with what looks like a painfully narrow crotch and a black tutu. On her feet are sneakers topped by scrunched-down black leg warmers.

Cher's exercise video constitutes just one in a wave of celebrity fitness videos, kick-started by Jane Fonda's iconic 1982 VHS, *Jane Fonda's Workout*. These videos are the banner product to emerge from a peculiar but perfect storm that hit in the final few decades of the last millennium: new interest in the details of celebrities' lives and bodies, a surge of interest in cardiovascular activity and—that old chestnut—social pressure for women to look a certain way. In the videos, the celebrities have the chance to demonstrate their lean physiques and physical stamina while ostensibly guiding acolytes down the path of the righteous.

The women in the '80s and '90s videos chirpily represent the optimism of post-Cold War American supremacy and, surely, the endorphins coursing through their bloodstreams. But Cher's announcement—that she doesn't like the thing she is about to do—belies the insidious underpinnings of the many industries devoted to making women into the way they are supposed to look.

In her book *This is Big*, Marisa Meltzer writes that women learn to "indulge in a morbid curiosity about each other through their bodies, and how we each measure up." Throughout the modern era, women have sought out ways to scratch this particular itch. Celebrity workout videos did the job for a while. Today, we primarily get our toxic, thrilling fix via the near-ubiquitous trend of celebrities posting videos of themselves exercising to Instagram. The aerobics and sweatbands are subbed for squats and leggings, to reflect the modern aesthetic. With the "how-to" aspect less pronounced, the preening intention of these videos is unmasked.

Our anxiety about weight today is primarily discussed through the prism of "health," meant to indicate concern about longevity rather than appearance. But how can we divorce exercise for health from exercise to meet unmeetable social expectations? Must we? It's an individual battle. But a home workout, undertaken as far away from Instagram as possible, might not be the worst way to burn off stress and live longer.

And for a body positive workout buddy, you could probably do worse than Cher.

4.

Directory

178 — 192

Peer Review

Harry Harris celebrates the legacy of enigmatic performer and "songwriter's songwriter" *Laura Nyro.*

Laura Nyro was a songwriter's songwriter, a prodigiously talented teenager from Connecticut, but inextricably linked to New York City. Between 1967 and 1971, she released five records of soul-meets-gospel-meets-show tunes-meets-rock 'n' roll, influencing everyone from Elton John to Carole King to Joni Mitchell.

I'm not sure I got Nyro as a kid, when her music would float through the walls of my bedroom from a record player elsewhere in our house in Wales. There'd be the odd flash of something. The climax of "Tom Cat Goodby"—where the shuffling pop of the first half segues into the terse, tense repetitive line: *I'm going to the country, gonna kill my lover man,* for instance. Her compositions and musical decisions felt like challenges, obstacles to overcome, and as someone mostly used to chugging four-four rock 'n' roll at that point, they often went over my head.

As a songwriter, I've been trying to unlearn a lot of those early, subconscious influences on what I do when I pick up a guitar, listening to music beyond my usual

sphere. Laura Nyro tunes always lingered in my memory, and I found that in revisiting her music as an adult, more of the abstractness began to crystallize: the opulence of the songs, the physicality of hearing her move around the piano keys and sing from deep in her chest. Nyro spoke about seeing music in terms of colors, shapes, textures, sensory things. Listening to her sing is like watching an artist throw colors onto a canvas, each movement informing the next.

There are a lot of descriptions of Nyro as being shy, or not tough enough for the hard-bitten world of the music industry. People cite that as the reason why her songs are best known in the hands of others. To me, it doesn't wash. She sounds like a star—like every breath and note and tempo change is a choice from someone who is deeply in love with her art. Watch her singing "Poverty Train" at Monterey in 1967. The camera is close, her eyes are darting around the room and her jet-black hair is indistinguishable from the darkness of the stage. Then there's her voice: colors, shapes, textures.

NEW YORK TENDABERRY
by Harry Harris

"New York Tendaberry" is a vignette of a song. The title track of Laura Nyro's 1969 record, it places you in a very specific version of New York. As she sings: *You look like a city, but you feel like religion to me.* Like much of the record, it's all about the relationship between Nyro's voice and her piano. Elsewhere she'll add woodwinds, drums, strings—creating a very precise and defined musical palette. Here, the two of them are alone, the song coming alive in the spaces where a piano chord lingers, like the city is taking a breath.

A fluff-free history of the pillow.

KATIE CALAUTTI

Object Matters

The next time you rest your weary head atop your memory foam, down, polyester or wool-stuffed pillow, try to avoid recalling the object's not-so-humble origins; you'll likely conjure nightmares. The main purpose of pillows, at first, was not for comfort. Back in early Mesopotamian civilization, the half-moon-shaped headrests were made of carved stone, and their main job was to keep insects out of the mouth, ears and nose of a person sleeping on the floor.

The Romans and Greeks brought comfort into the equation, perfecting the pillow's ability to support the head, neck and spine by stuffing cloth with feathers or straw. Initially, the bolsters were seen as a sign of wealth, though the general populace adopted them over time, especially as an accessory brought to a place of worship to cushion knees while praying. But solid pillows prevailed elsewhere for longer. In ancient China, for example—where it was believed that soft pillows pulled energy from the body—lavishly painted ceramic versions were de rigueur through the 14th century; materi-

als like jade, bamboo and bronze were common as well. The industrial revolution brought with it sleeping platforms, and softer pillows became mass-produced and more affordable. With the cotton boom in 19th-century America, the stuffing became more mold- and vermin-resistant; suddenly, pillows were no longer a luxury, they were a necessity. The Victorians, predictably, delighted in—and popularized—the concept of decorative pillows, and by the mid-1900s, the invention of polyester filling introduced stuffing that maintained its shape.

Now, one can purchase a pillow to suit just about any need—they're no longer solely touted for optimal sleep, but for emotional and physical health. Body-shaped pillows mimic a partner, cooling gel inserts keep sleepers chill in hot conditions, maternity pillows support the contours of mamas-to-be and travel pillows prop us up while flying. Smart pillows can even mimic sunshine or play music to help us rise. The downside of the pillow's newfound comfort is, of course, that each morning's parting is a sweet sorrow.

Cult Rooms

Throughout history, philosophers physicians and the state have all muscled in on the gym.

You might think of the gym as a modern invention, with its metal equipment both shiny and matte, hi-tech performance fabrics and electronic machines whirring away—but you'd only be half right.

Indeed, the modern gym has its roots on the beaches of Southern California, where GIs returning from World War II congregated for group exercise en plein air. Through sun-kissed fitness sessions, they sought camaraderie, sex appeal and an escape from the humdrum existences of their parents and grandparents, says Eric Chaline, author of *The Temple of Perfection: A History of the Gym*, on the phone from his home in London.

But the location of the first gyms—or gymnasia—will be obvious to anyone with a passing interest in etymology: ancient Greece. Literally translated to "the place where nakedness happens," including but not necessarily limited to exercise, the gymnasium was "without exaggeration the most important institution in the ancient city-state," says Chaline.

Gymnasia developed in the 8th century BCE as training facilities: for military skills as well as for Greek Olympiads, where competitors vied for glory in events including foot races, equestrian events, wrestling, javelin and discus. Like much of life in ancient Greece, people trained alfresco, in "courtyards surrounded by porticos, within which were changing rooms, the cadets' mess, massage and oiling rooms, baths, and classrooms," according to Chaline.

And what classrooms these were. Because the gymnasia's raison d'être was to prepare elite boys for civic life, an education in philosophy was considered as important as martial skills and a well-toned physique. The three public gyms outside Athens, Chaline says, spawned the Platonic, Cynic and Peripatetic schools of philosophy, the latter founded by Aristotle. Philosophers whose names still ring out today lectured in the

Photography: François Coquerel.
Architects: Le Coadic & Scotto

porticos of these gymnasia. Once Greece was conquered by the Romans, Greek boys no longer had to be skilled in military tactics. Physical fitness fell out of fashion until the Renaissance, when some doctors again became interested in athletics. But, says Chaline, no actual gyms opened: "The ruling classes of the Renaissance were too busy dying in wars, murdering one another, succumbing to plague, or eating and drinking themselves to death" to worry about missing leg day. The social and educational reform of the Enlightenment reignited interest in physical activity. The first post-Renaissance gyms opened in the German states around the turn of the 19th century. These reflected the classical model, with fixed equipment in line with what we see today in gymnastics: parallel bars, chinning bars, vaulting horses and rings. Also like their ancient forebears, they were open-air, presumably presenting an added climatic challenge to German athletes.

STEPHANIE D'ARC TAYLOR

Bad Idea:
Dance Marathons

The Depression-era craze with deadly consequences.

Popular entertainment is often powered by schadenfreude. In Roman times, spectators packed stadiums to gleefully observe as people were dismembered by lions. More recently, the explosion of reality television has given popcorn-munchers the chance to watch people make themselves sick from eating too many cockroaches or undergo extreme plastic surgery to look like flash-in-the-pan celebrities.

Depression-era dance marathons are the 1930s counterpart to 2000s reality television. These spectacles began innocently enough as dance contests in the 1920s, when long-haul dance events trod the fine, fascinating line between sexily scandalous and over-the-top outrageous. Alma Cummings kick-started the craze in 1923, wearing holes in her shoes from 27 straight hours of dancing in a Manhattan ballroom. Within three weeks, her record had been broken at least nine times by two-steppers across the country.

When the stock market crashed in 1929, what had started as light-footed romps quickly morphed into entertainment events bordering on the sadistic. Depression-era dancers, lured by regular meals and cash prizes that regularly exceeded a farmer's annual sal-ary, were governed by rules set by speculative promoters eager to put on ever-more addictively macabre shows for their audiences.

Breaks were only permitted for medical or hygienic purposes, or attention-grabbing gambits like elimination sprints, mud wrestling, or compulsory wedding ceremonies. Often, sleeping was forbidden unless one partner kept moving, which meant that dancers took turns slumped against their partners in what doesn't appear to be very restful slumber.

Worse, the marathons began stretching into weeks, testing contestants' physical and mental endurance. One Seattle woman attempted suicide after placing fifth at the end of a 19-day competition. The city of Boston outlawed dance marathons when a man dropped dead after dancing for 87 straight hours. But spectators, eager for a distraction from their own troubles, continued to pay entrance fees day after day.

World War II was many things to many people—not least a massive creator of jobs. Once people had something real to do again, spectator dance marathons died out. Of course, our inability to look away from awkwardness, discomfort, and worse, remains alive and well.

BELLA GLADMAN

Last Night

What did singer Tyson McVey do with her evening?

Thirty-one-year-old Tyson McVey is a singer from west London. Music is in her genes: Her parents are veteran hit-makers Neneh Cherry and Cameron McVey, and her younger sister, Mabel, won the Brit Award for British Female Solo Artist earlier this year. Family is key for McVey. She works full time for her mother as a PA and on social media, and she's (temporarily) moved back home until she buys a place that can be her own "little universe."

BG: *What did you get up to last night?* **TM:** I went to see my little sister, Mabel, perform. She sold out the Hammersmith Apollo—unreal! After, I stayed up late with my cousins and auntie. They're over from Sweden and we had a feast in my room, where they're staying on the floor.

BG: *Is that your childhood bedroom?* **TM:** No. I grew up all over the place, between London, Spain and Sweden. My favorite childhood bedroom was in Spain—it was my own domain, and the first time I hadn't had to share with my older sister, Naima.

BG: *What's your room like now?* **TM:** There's a lot of other people's stuff in there! On my bedside table, I have a Le Labo candle that I stole from my sister, and my gold necklace: I've been collecting charms for it for 16 years, but it gets tangled in my hair, so I take it off. I would say a book, but I always end up watching *Love Island* before I go to sleep.

BG: *Are your evenings usually spent with your family?* **TM:** It's been lovely having dinners at home with my parents. I listened to an amazing podcast by Chantelle Lewis, a sociologist, on the black mixed-race experience. Being mixed myself, I'd never heard someone talk about it in this way. I told them about it at home one night. My dad said, "Let's put it on," so we listened together and discussed it for hours. It was really sweet.

BG: *Your song "White/Seven" feels perfect for an intimate gathering. After-party at your place?* **TM:** I love a party. I'm always the last man standing. I never say, "Come back to mine!" though. I'm always like, "Where are we going?"

The poet and novelist avoiding definitive endings.

BELLA GLADMAN

Ocean Vuong

Vietnamese American writer Ocean Vuong's debut poetry collection, *Night Sky with Exit Wounds*, won multiple awards, and his debut novel, *On Earth We're Briefly Gorgeous*, hit *The New York Times* bestseller list. His work is semiautobiographical, exploring and illuminating a lesser-known America through a queer, immigrant perspective. In 2019, he was awarded a "genius" grant of $625,000 by the MacArthur Foundation. He says that means lots of things, including more pizza for his MFA students at the University of Massachusetts Amherst.

BG: *You're based in Northampton, Massachusetts. What's it like?* **OV:** We have four bookstores in a two-block radius. I've never lived anywhere that has that, even New York, where I lived for 11 years. I don't miss any intellectual rigor here. There's a perfect balance of contemplation, proximity to nature, and a long history of grassroots activism, queer feminists and women-centric thinking (being the home of Sylvia Plath, where her papers are held). It's a different, intellectual, quirky, queer hub of thinking—ideal for me, as opposed to the city. Things are smaller and slower, more deliberate. That pace is akin to sentence-making.

BG: *You write in experimental forms. How do you know when you've finished?* **OV:** You keep going until what you add to the work becomes less than what's already there. It might take weeks, maybe months before you realize, "All right. This is it." There's no finish line. *On Earth's* fragmented structure is an attempt to resist the anxiety of production and completion. Particularly in the West, we're asked, "When are you going to finish your novel/essay/article?" We're obsessed with the finite. It took queer writers, like Maggie Nelson, to unsettle that. By writing in a fragmentary nature, it's a refusal to complete, and thus reduce it.

BG: *Having written both poetry and fiction, how do they compare?* **OV:** Poems bring me more joy than novels do. The novel was important as it forced me to stay in that world with more longevity. I couldn't turn away. You write a good line in a poem, and you're like, "Oh, that's enough! Into the drawer it goes!" But in a novel, you've got to make sure your characters leave the room, use the restroom. That was a great challenge.

BG: *What's it like to win a grant that frees you from financial constraints for five years?* **OV:** It means that emergencies in my extended family are now taken care of. That alone is such incredible freedom; before, I was helpless. So far, I've had a successful book of poems and a successful novel—that's super cool. But usually, it's not like that. The next one is bound to suck! I've got to hunker down to make something that isn't terrible, lazy or pretentious, and I'm free to do that.

BG: *How do you feel about your book, now that it's out in the world?* **OV:** Once upon a time, you'd carry stories with you, and they'd change every time they were told. Now writing a book is like taking a photograph of your mind. *On Earth* is a snapshot of March 2019, when I made my final edits. To be honest, if I had another crack at the book today, I would probably change about five to ten percent. Ten years from now, who knows? I could throw it all out. Yet, I needed to be that person who wrote that book then to become my future self now. I didn't know *On Earth* would take off like this; it's bizarre! Because a strange, experimental text like that has been well-received, I feel liberated to be more daring, more ambitious.

The starred clues in this issue's crossword incorporate dance moves into common phrases.

ANNA GUNDLACH

Crossword

ACROSS

1. Joe that won't give you the jitters
6. "Frozen" queen
10. Nukes in the microwave
14. Nuke testing site, once
15. Brunch, e.g.
16. 1973 Toni Morrison bestseller
17. Tropical ocean ray
18. Key near Alt
19. "The Father of Economics" Smith
20. * Fashion publication since 1892
23. Had brunch
25. Last of 26
26. High-pressure hosp. rooms
27. Cleanser with the slogan "Hasn't scratched yet!"
30. Necessitates
34. Highly-contested election territory
37. Unimportant problem to pick
38. Late bedtime
39. Kept out of sight
40. Playful water critter
42. ___ Tin Tin (former dog star)
43. * Spicy condiment made from tomatillos and green peppers
45. "…and that's the truth!"
48. Greet with respect
49. Cracker container
50. "___ the season…"
52. URL portion
53. * Intentionally make someone's situation worse, idiomatically
59. Upward movement
60. Irish for "Ireland"
61. Bucatini or orzo
64. Societal problems
65. Humorist Bombeck
66. Move out of the way of
67. Poetic praise
68. Loch with a famous monster
69. Kind of movement leading to the answers to this puzzle's starred clues

DOWN

1. Big stopper of water movement
2. Character in a Greek play?
3. Labor-saving
4. Woman in a choir
5. Certain symbol of the LGBT pride movement
6. Show's host
7. "I can take care of it for you!"
8. Gilbert of "Roseanne"
9. Kid's exclamation after cleaning their dinner plate
10. Glamorous Gabor
11. German car manufacturer
12. It might get hatched
13. Interchangeable
21. Action movie weapons
22. Word with "collection" or "movement"
23. Soak up
24. Off-campus local resident
28. Ortiz of "Ugly Betty"
29. Studio with a roaring lion mascot
30. Airport takeoff approximations: abbr.
31. Sticks one's nose into
32. Wasn't forthright with
33. City road
35. The item over there
36. Feel sick
40. Eggs, to a biologist
41. Business card no.
43. Number of pawns on a chess board
44. Part of AMA
46. Be completely preoccupied (with)
47. Negative word
50. The fine print
51. Stores that sell meatballs and furniture
53. Threesome
54. Feral
55. Tiny thing on a map
56. Put on the team
57. Tech that comes in Air and Pro versions
58. Bean variety famously mentioned in "The Silence of the Lambs"
62. Little facial movement
63. Fruity drink suffix

HARRY HARRIS

Correction

There's no such thing as being "right-brained."

For over a century, people have gladly filed themselves into two camps: left-brained and right-brained. If your left brain is dominant, you're logical and methodical. If your right brain has control of the wheel, you're creative, emotional and artsy.

Certain parts of the brain do control certain things. Language, for instance, is controlled by the left side. It was this discovery, made by neuroscientists Paul Broca and Carl Wernicke in the 19th century, that led to a wider Victorian obsession with "dual-brain theory." Robert Louis Stevenson played upon it in his novella *Strange Case of Dr. Jekyll and Mr. Hyde*, in which the protagonists—one good, one evil—turn out to be the two personalities of one man.

It's perhaps unsurprising that the Victorians took to the theory so readily, given this was also the era when phrenology—a pseudoscience that linked personality traits to the shape of people's skulls—flourished. Much like phrenology, dual-brain theory brought its own biases: the logical left brain was associated with masculinity, the emotional right with femininity, left with whiteness, right with supposed savagery. It doesn't take a genius to work out what was going on. Given that the brain is so complex, it is ironic that a theory that reduces it to such a neat binary ever took off. Believers feel, however, that it intuitively makes sense. Like horoscopes and Buzz-Feed quizzes, the myth also gives people a convenient way to define themselves, and to associate with others. In truth, the brain always works as one. Its two sides are connected by 250 million nerve fibers known as the corpus callosum, which send messages from one to the other almost instantaneously. This is why apps or puzzles that purport to "train" one half of your brain are pulling a fast one. Both sides of your brain are always working equally as hard whether you're writing a song or solving an equation.

A 2013 study from the University of Utah looked at the brain scans of more than 1,000 young people and divided the brain into 7,000 regions to determine whether one side of the brain was more active than the other side. No evidence of "sidedness" was found.

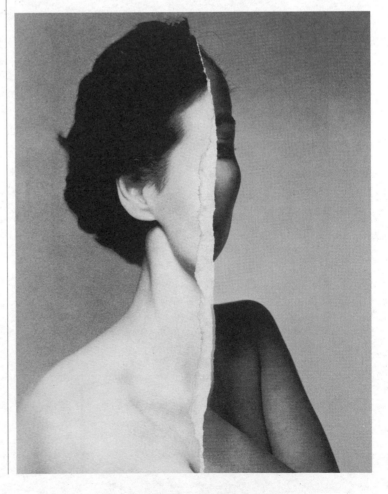

NEW WORKS.

Kizu Table Lamp

The Kizu Table Lamp displays a weightless balancing act composed of two contrasting sculptural forms, where the illusion of gravity creates tension within the piece. The curved shapes initiate a calming effect and the kissing point of material and function creates an object in complete harmony.